THE UNSTUFFY DESCRIPTIVE LEADERSHIP BOOK

VELMA OSBORNE

THE UNSTUFFY DESCRIPTIVE LEADERSHIP BOOK

Inclusive of Language Usage, Networking, Theories, Culture as well as Funding of Business Enterprises

The Unstuffy Descriptive Leadership Book

Published in the United States of America

ISBN: 978-1-949362-93-0 (*sc*)
978-1-949362-92-3 (*e*)

Library of Congress Control Number: 2018957028

Published by Stonewall Press
4800 Hampden Lane, Suite 200, Bethesda, MD 20814 USA
1.888.334.0980 | www.stonewallpress.com

1. Business
2. Reference Books
19.02.04

Contents

GOOD LEADERSHIP STARTS WITH TEAMWORK

I WOULD LOVE TO HEAR FROM YOU. LET'S BUILD A COMMUNITY & SHARE SOME IDEAS.

JOIN ME IN SOCIAL MEDIA. HERE ARE THE AVENUES WHERE WE CAN TALK AND HELP EACH OTHER

Velma Osborne

Leaderauthor

The Unstuffy Descriptive Leadership Book

revosborne2@gmail.com

Introduction

THIS BOOK CAPTURES THE depth of leaders. Some fundamentals will be given so that further intricacies will be understood. This book is flexibly useful for those who are in business, working on projects, managers, recreation entrepreneurs, administrators or students with an interest in leadership. Even well-established businesses that desire motivation or new ideas can receive some benefit from reading this book.

Especially, quiet people sometimes have the erroneous idea that leadership or management in its many forms is impossible to attempt. Study can change their opinion of themselves and give them a realistic view of their potentials. Some extroverts actually entered business with the euphoric idea that they would be a business magnet only to fail in a short period of time. This informative book handles a wide range of challenges that health facilities, businesses, schools and clubs have to face. This book encapsulates materials from numerous references plus expertise from my unique background that will stimulate personal growth to most that read it. Author's quantitative and qualitative values in the form of quotes will be shown. Also, the reasons for leaders', business owners' or managers' usage of consultants for unbiased ideas or criticism will be taught. It will be shown that some least expected persons can be excellent advisors.

It also extends to Church leaders who may choose to depend much more on God solely rather than any leadership style. The reason church leaders need knowledge of methodologies is because God uses what you know. He can give you the appropriate place or time to apply various styles with corresponding techniques. Additionally, many employees or church staffs have to understand their managers, team leaders, club leaders or heads of auxiliaries. Staff personnel or those with only membership status, many times cannot see the reasoning behind some of the changes the upper echelon make. Anguish, misery and dislike of a leader because of a decision made, can be minimized if one understands more about leadership. In other words ignorance can be dispelled and at least some personal irritations or anguish can be alleviated.

Today no one has to be a lone ranger struggling down the aisle of entangled business problems. There is possibly something in this endeavor that can jar one's mind into inventiveness by showing a relationship between an individual's life and business experiences with others. There is nothing like being motivated into performing self-analysis by reading about the successes and failures of others. Alterations can be made in business after successful techniques are known.

The variety of authors' immensely different approaches to various aspects of business will expand the readers mind. Never will I forget Joyce Myers book, "*The Battle Field is in the Mind*". It is apparent that certain cerebral stations in our minds have never been turned on. Expansion of your thinking can come from different sources. Business leaders that started with next to nothing and those that had wealthy parents or relatives can pass down successful modalities. Shackles can break off minds and more individuals can be fresh to go.

The topics that were handled in the authors' books listed in the bibliography range the gamut from very simple and easily applied to the complex. Some of the books have dialogues that only a corporation or firm that has almost reached their summit would have need of such complicated procedures. Many times changes for businesses that are higher up are the only ones that have the collateral or actual cash to advance to optimal levels. Not to worry, there are very simple inexpensive changes to a business that will benefit many. More fortitude, and new ideas rather than much more financial aid or increase in staff will help improve a firm. In this book such changes as attitude, brain storming, rewarding staff for good work and innovations, can change the façade as well as inner workings of a business or a club. A positive playing field instead of a tension-filled ready to fail business environment can be ameliorated many times by learnt behavioral changes.

Given here is a synopsis of the seven chapters that will give you an orientation that will enable you to extract beneficial ideas that will enhance comprehension of the aim of this book. Chapter one gives a baseline understanding of leadership by giving the character traits as well as the definition of leadership.

Chapter two is demonstrative of the personal input of leaders that nurture tensions or do not. The attitudes of leaders and their followers will be addressed. What happens if behavior changes of the leaders or followers are introduced? In other words retraining or training for the first time should be implemented for better results!

Chapter three highlights organizational leadership theories. Each methodology has its place. Some theories can simultaneously work with another depending on the context of situations or special events that occur in the work place. Explanations of various scenarios will be given in order to demonstrate appropriate application of these theories. Results will be given so that one can visualize whether this approach is needed for your corporation, church, school or club.

Chapter four gives a comparison analysis of the differences between family firms and other businesses. In other words there are advantages and disadvantages in family firms and the same goes for other businesses. Adjustments in some cases can be made to increase profits or insure the longevity of family businesses that could be understood by its members. It necessitates comparison analysis with other businesses. Perhaps at times corporations and other businesses can attain more success if there were more comradery that sometimes is apparent in family businesses. Trainings and studying of the two prototypes can be interesting and many times profitable for both. Consultants are usually used to aid in the explorations of these matters.

Chapter five handles the mechanics of every business, facility, faith-based organization, school or club. It is speech production and language usage which is inclusive of dialect differences. Many times the manner in which something is said out shines the content. The mechanics of speech needs to be observed in order to determine if it is adequate enough to bear fruit. One's language usage, as well as dialect must be scrutinized for the same reason. When sale pitches, seminars, trainings or presentations are given, changes may have to be made in order for the business, school or club to prosper.

Chapter six delves into types of groups, funding, and the results of targeting specific audiences. In other words the demographics of the audiences in business, school, faith-based organization or club will affect how it can be funded and dealt with on all other levels. For example a whole food store may donate healthy food to an affair given by an exercise club that saves them the money of having to buy food themselves!

Chapter seven which is providential leadership is unique in that many times belief in God supersedes making money. In other words there is more of a concern for a business deal to be satisfactory for the manager, staff as well as consumers. Certain "cut throat" sales techniques many times will not be used but instead prayer will be instituted in order to receive what believers deem to be a supernatural turn around in favor of a business. Specific faith based entities in general must be understood both by who they extend business to as well as from whom they receive commodities. It many times requires study on both sides.

This book has a wealth of business and leadership information set forth in an unstuffy manner. Unnecessary time is not wasted rereading information in order to get anything usable out of it. Application is the gift of the author who is a Speech and Language Pathologist as well as a Preacher-Chaplain. Success for all types of leaders is the salient thought. If leaders sought out the areas of the book that is needed for success of their type of business and implement changes, deletions or additions offered, successes will begin to blossom.

CHAPTER I

Basics of Leadership

A. Signs of a Leader

A DECISION WAS MADE by me to make an abrupt start on this informative leadership theme in order to have a baseline for the balance of the material which follows. *Merriam Webster Desk Dictionary* (Merriam Webster Inc. Philippines1995) readily credits leaders to be the following:

1. One that guides on a way; One who is in front; One who tends toward a definite result.
2. A guiding or directing head, as of an army, movement, or political group.
3. Persons who direct operations, activity or performance as of an orchestra.

John Maxwell's definition of a leader in his book, *Developing the Leader*, uses simply the word influential as a descriptive term for a leader.[1] In other words a leader necessitates being powerful enough to have a following. In my estimation a leader of the Student Government of a school could not have gotten that position if he or she were not popular. Leaders of fund raisers could not hold this position if they were not beneficially, handy in respect to financial dealings.

Personally, my viewpoint deems a leader to be the person or animal that is at the beginning of a line or in a launching position. When it is a person he or she is liked, tolerated or hated. Unlike supervisors they devise original plans and rules or supplement plans that are already in place (John Maxwell's book). Supervisors put into action regulations and plans that are assigned to them by leaders. In other words supervisors are trainers and enforcers of their staffs' job details. Leaders are the individuals that are formulators of job descriptions or enhancers. In my estimation they are innovative movers and shakers that are able to adapt to changing situations or environments. They are strong persons who are able to pass on changes to supervisors or directly orchestrate new variations to job specifics themselves.

In order for the term leader to move into a tangible context for readers here is an example. Years ago when I was eighteen years of age, I went on a trip to Quebec, Canada. For the first time in my life I went horseback riding. Being that I was a city person it was indeed an adventurous first try. At that time I was not cognizant of the fact that there was such a thing as a lead

---

1 John Maxwell, *Developing the Leader Within You* (Nashville: Thomas Nelson, 2005), 1

horse. Fifth in line was my position when the first horse took off. All I knew how to do was hold on tight to the reign which was not a problem until the lead horse rode through bushes. My horse to my chagrin pursued him. Of course I received a few little scratches. That was not anything compared to what happened later. The lead horse decided to cross a street that had no traffic until it was my horse's turn to cross. When my horse stepped into the street it observed a car coming toward him and suddenly reared up on his hind legs with me hanging on for dear life. An intelligent decision was made by me after that fiasco. I would never go for a horseback ride again! Obviously, if it were a good human leader encountering a surprise occurrence there would be a strategy in place due to adaptable past experiences in life. Effective intervention that would avert disastrous results would be immediately implemented when unexpected events occur.

In Maxwell's book, he voiced an admiration for an author who studied birds called cranes. He learned that cranes rotate leadership. This natural occurrence by cranes seems to be a pattern that could be and is successfully followed by some human beings. At this point in time I am going to make a comparison analysis in order to bring out the importance of the study of cranes. It came to me that the crane type of rotation of leadership scheme of things is used in the United States government. A President can only serve two terms. Senators, Congressmen, Mayors and Governors all have term limitations. If people are dissatisfied with their leaders they vote them out in one or two terms of office. Since different people have different strengths, weaknesses, influencers and belief systems, curtailment of their functioning many times can be advantageous. Also leaders may have vastly varying connections with people that can make things happen at their discretion on a large scale. Other countries at times suffer for decades with a dictator or kingly dynasty running their country with no let up. Hurrah for the implementation of the crane's successful rotation of leadership type of governmental structure.

B. The Highpoints of Leaders

Some unique or stronger assets must exist in a leader in order to differentiate him or her from most other individuals. Their differences and strengths give them the ability to call the shots. In the book, *Developing the Leader within You*, was mentioned a personality trait that struck me as being an extremely important quality. It is an effective mannerism that can improve every function in a leader's life. "Discipline", is the targeted behavior. Featured in the beginning of Bruce Kasanoff book, *How to Self-Promote Without Being a Jerk*, are additional personality traits that are inherent or acquired by leaders.[2] His listings are explicit and very easily understood. These characteristics are as follows: generous, expert, trustworthy, open minded and persistent. Discipline, Maxwell's character trait will begin the discussion followed by Kasanoff's personality attributes.

Discipline

Delving right into the personality trait namely discipline, I will put the term into the context of a situation. Many

---

2 Bruce Kasanoff, *How to Self-Promote Without Being a Jerk* (West-Point: Now Possible, 2014), i-iv

people are cognizant of the fact that a leader that is late all the time usually will have some employees that are careless with time also. Here is an example of what happens when staff members are not given strict guidelines about time. This occurred in an elementary school in which I used to be employed. The Principal who is the leader of the school chose to come in late in the mornings and stay late into early evenings. The result was that classes were not picked up on time from the cafeteria or yard in the mornings. The children began actual work fifteen to twenty minutes after the hour school was supposed to start. After the school received a low rating a study was conducted to see what could be done to make the school run more efficiently. About 6 top teachers in the school were chosen to make recommendations for improvement in the school. Also comparisons were made with schools that were top performers as well as other countries that were more successful educating children than the United States. Whatever the findings were it changed my Principal. The Principal met with all of the teachers, therapists, paraprofessionals, aids and other staff. Rigid rules were laid down that required getting to work approximately fifteen minutes to a half hour before the work day began in order to be teaching or doing administrative work exactly at start time. Letters would be placed in the file of teachers and other staff if they chose not to abide with the new rule. Additionally teachers had to attend mandatory workshops during one prep period per week on time. Suddenly to the staffs chagrin the Principal would suddenly show up on various floors peering into classrooms, and offices observing whether work was going on exactly or close as possible to the hour. The staff indeed worked much harder for the same pay due to the Principal herself use of time economy. The teachers, paraprofessionals as well as other staff members complained and called the Principal's new intense scrutiny of the staff unnecessary micro management. Well unnecessary micro management or not it continued even with the knowledge of the Teachers Union (UFT) until the end of the year! The corrective measures put in place for disciplining tardy staff as well as the principal her self being on the job early in the morning deterred disobedience. At the end of the year the school rating went up enough to take it off the failing list. Since the Mayor and the Chancellor of New York Schools were threatening to close down the school this small gain was a huge victory.

Generous

In review of the Bruce Kasanoff's listing of personality traits the pin pong effect technique will be used in order to display information in a usable format. Generosity will be addressed at this time. Leaders of gambling establishments in Atlantic City (CEO's) are aware of the fact that giving to their customers reaps a handsome reward for the Casinos. An acquaintance of mine told me that she enjoyed going to Atlantic City. Her sole purpose in going was to play the gambling machine (One Armed Bandit) which is filed with change. Happily she exclaimed, "When you get on the private buses to go to the Casinos they give every passenger ten dollars' worth of quarters to use playing the one arm bandit." This news surprised me. Evidently the leaders of these establishments discovered that giving motivates people to spend much more. Starting them off with ten dollars is an incentive for them to splurge later. Apparently the CEO's are either Actuaries or have Actuaries as their main consultants on staff. They are aware and constantly alerted to the history of spending patterns that gamblers follow. Most possibly statistical proportions and ratios are in place that average out the amount of people that can win as well as the demographics of the individuals that play. It is highly probable that people are studied so that they understand which type of person will spend the least and the most. The number of people that can possibly hit the jackpot is known beforehand. In other words the CEO's are smiling because they know the house is stacked against the public. Some customers win a small amount at first which entices them to play more after all they started with free money. "What the heck," some gamblers may be saying. As the gambling continues what at first was partially attributed to the free money caused the creation of innumerable dreams to occur. "If I win, that car will be mine. If I win, I can go on vacation. If I win, I can get a house for the family. If I win, I can retire from that job that I cannot stand. If I win, I can get that woman I want." Like conversation schizophrenia, one wrong motivation to gamble gives birth to more gambling instead of incomplete topic development. Now the psychological term compulsive gambler comes into play. Remember all of this vicious cycle started with a generous gift of ten dollars. Recently some genius leader introduced online gambling. There are also some enticing free offers to get the public gambling online. The establishments earn even more because the consumers do not have the expense of traveling to a casino, eating in restaurants or paying for a hotel bill. They use some or all of the extra money to gamble. The leaders that strategized online gambling are most probably already extremely rich.

It seemed apparent to the naked eye when an owner of a restaurant advertised, all you can eat for a flat rate that it would be a losing financial battle. It is noteworthy that nothing much can be made per customer if you allow customers to eat as much as they desire. Also I observed when I frequented one of these types of restaurants the fattest people that I have ever seen in my life consuming food there! Most certainly due to the generous gesture of the owners (leaders) customers spread the word that you can get more for your money. Employers spread the word to their employees; church groups spread the word to their parishioners; families have their special events there, and on and on and on. These entrepreneurs that begun this generous gesture must have been successful because other buffets began to pop up in many states. My mouth is watering right now just thinking about *The Golden Corral* and other buffets that allow feasting. Enough money must be made because most of their seating remains fairly full while other types of restaurants at times are empty or sparsely filled. Hurrah, for the restaurants that poor to middle income families can afford to go to due to a generosity scheme. Their owners I am sure are thankful for their success and money made due to the increase in the number of patrons.

A generous leader can also give ideas to other leaders in order to aid them in becoming successful with their endeavor. The enthusiast many times will not get anything helpful back from the person he assisted. At a later date someone else may give the supporter a helping hand by giving them referrals, or materials. Also information to get financial assistance to branch out may be given. Kansanoff calls such kind leaders promoters of others. Evidently generous leaders radiate a certain glow that others notice and are motivated to aid or give valuable information.

Looking back to nineteen ninety-nine when my husband and I bought a building to house the homeless, I remember all the numerous problems. These occurrences caused me some sleepless nights. It was not the homeless men and women that caused the biggest problems. It was the person that I used as the director of the program. She demonstrated gross incompetence to the extent that my husband and I had to close the building. We sacrificed in order to provide for those who were disenfranchised and received trouble in return. But while we were still in that dilemma someone who was a friend of the faulty director gave my husband and I information on how to obtain a non-profit corporation. We successfully received our 501(c)(3) which is used for other types of mission work and endeavors. So our efforts were not totaled by a director who lost her focus and mismanaged our building. In the end we narrowly avoided foreclosure and were able to sell the building for a profit. We also received good reports from some of the people who stayed in our building for the year that the program functioned. A few were working or attending school. Some others functioned in programs geared for restoration of drug addicts as well as those who have not been employed for years. It is their good report which made my heart glad in addition to the formation of the non–profit corporation.

Expert

A leader is an expert in his or her own area of concentration. In their area of specialty, the ability to persuade, teach or demonstrate to others how to perform a particular task is evident. Being that most people have to visit an eye specialist their particular expertise came to my mind. A lead ophthalmologist formulated a method to prevent pressure or alleviate high pressures that already exist in eyes. This technique prevents decreasing vision due to a disease called glaucoma. The cause of the pressure build up is due to fluid not circulating properly through the drain in the eye (Current Medical Diagnosis and Treatment).[3] Previously only various prescription eye drops were used to slow down or stop pressure build up in eyes. Use of these drops alone sometimes resulted in a downhill fight against becoming legally blind to totally blind. Presently a procedure by leading eye surgeons is used that offers some patients a laser treatment before any or much vision is lost. The ophthalmologist actually puts a tiny opening in a targeted section of the eye with a laser that decreases pressure build up by seventy–five percent. Of course these expert leaders in their field train doctors and give them the go ahead to advise patients to use their advanced laser skill to save vision. What is really "cool" about laser surgery is unlike other eye surgery it is performed on outpatient basis and requires very little recovery! What a wonderful breakthrough expert eye doctors are now spreading that decreases the possibility of terrible vision loss. I am only sorry that my own mother died at the wonderful age of ninety-one with her mind but totally blind for seven years resulting from glaucoma. Unfortunately this new innovation

---

3 Maxine A. Papadakis, Stephen J. McPhee, Associated Editor Michael W. Rabow, *Current Medical Diagnosis and Treatment* (USA McGraw Hill-Education, 2014), 174

was not on the market in her day! The original leaders in the field of eye surgery that devised the laser technique are now most likely extremely rich. So many thousands of people are grateful due to the saving of their sight.

In the past public schools used an incredible amount of paper for memorandums for staff alone. They also sponsored numerous workshops and gave teachers packets of information for their perusal afterwards. Additionally thousands of attendance books were given to teachers along with progress report sheets for formal documentation of Special Education student's advancement or regression. Millions of dollars were spent yearly by our government until the state budget allotment for paper usage for schools was drastically cut. Some genius leaders in the area of economics as well as computer experts proposed a plan where student attendance is now accomplished on the computer along with progress reports. Of course many times reports and other computerized charting of students attributes, progress and attendance have to be printed out. Guess what, teachers many times have to bring their own paper to print their work out. So the government is no longer stuck with an exorbitant bill. To the chagrin of the teachers they have to buy the paper so their salary has to stretch further. Additionally, teachers are instructed by the administrators of the schools that they must go on the Department of Education's website and look for weekly or monthly memorandums that will come in their individual e-mails so that they can learn about upcoming events, materials or information to give out to parents. In this manner thousands of more dollars are saved by going paperless!

Trustworthy

In continuing I am lifting up the value of trustworthy leaders. Years ago I stopped shopping at a small boutique because the owner mixed used clothing with new. Kasanoff gives credence to the trust factor by his statement, "A person who respects authenticity is a leader." Disappointment hit me like a ton of bricks after I tried on the item I bought at home. The elastic inside the waist band was twisted due to previous wear and an area of the garment was slightly soiled. When apparels are bought you like to feel it is clean and spanking new. Realization that a switch had been made was causative of an immediate countenance change accompanied by anger. Never will I shop in that store again I ranted! Certainly others have made the same vow once a used clothing switch was made. Either a decrease in clientele will force the store to be honest or they will make less money or possibly be forced to close.

An on the job deceitful practice was highlighted in a chapter in Geiser's book *Work Happy.*[4] She labeled it, "What employees never forget." What staff cannot forget is when a boss takes the credit for the staffs' work or ideas. This undermining behavior is due to the leader's feeling of intimidation. Of course it is obvious the staff may no longer work as hard or readily give advice due to their distrust of their boss. A "happy camper" that is rewarded for their additions will have a much better attitude towards his superiors than one that is saddened by being purposely overshadowed.

---

4 Jill Geiser, *Work Happy: What Great Bosses Know* (NYC: Center Street: Hachette Book Group, 2012) 29

Another problem exhibited by management is acting one way with the staff and another way with their superiors. Here's a personal example. After twenty-five years of receiving a satisfactory rating as a Speech Teacher my principal was coerced by a government budget reduction to illegally get rid of some top paid veteran teachers. Expecting the Union Leader in my school to advocate for me gave me solace. To my chagrin I discovered she acted one way with me and another with the principal of the school who gave me illegal gym duty (A tactic to undermine my professional status as a Speech and Language Pathologist). This duty was causative of terrible stress and anguish. Trust in the lead union representative went out of the window. I had to call and send constant e-mails to her superior the head of the Union's entire Speech Department. Not only was my job on the line but also my pension that I was due to receive upon retirement. The head of the UFT's Speech Department was over two thousands Speech Teachers. After investigation of my good record and a dialogue with the school based useless representative, she met with the principal and my job was spared! Most importantly the principal was forced to respect me. Although I still spoke to the immediate Union leader I never had the trust to tell her anything of substance again.

Open Minded

Being open minded is a quality of a flexible leader. He or she probably holds a "there is more than one way to accomplish a task," mentality. Even though seeing someone else's point of view and putting it into action, may cause one to jump through hoops or crawl through tunnels they are willing to give it a try. Chris Widener in his book, *Leadership rules: How to become a Leader You Want to be*, speaks of a man that at first was not open-minded.[5] Mike Keller one of the managers of a large factory in Chicago, learned to be a much better business leader from an improbable source. He was demoted from his position in the parent company in Chicago and sent to a hick town called Creek in Texas. He was told he had shortcomings compared to the other leaders. He thought predictably that he should have been sent to an executive leadership program but instead he was forced to go to Texas. Apparently, because he is used to business as usual Mike was incapable of realizing that "hands on" experience could be much more fruitful.

Mike remorsefully took his teenager football player son and relocated to the smaller Texas Plant. After he began managing the plant he found the workers were immobile and unaccepting of the changes he desired implemented. Mike recognized that their pay was good and the retired manager did not do anything to motivate them to perform at their best for numerous years. He needed a consultation with a knowledgeable person. He was advised by a parent on his son's team to be mentored by his football coach. "He's the best leader in town," he was told. Mike was amazed that someone could recommend someone that was not functioning in an academic domain. He voiced, "Logan is only a coach!" Coach Logan's team won seventeen out of twenty-six championships. He found out the coaches goal was not only winning championships but mainly making champions. His goal was to develop boys to be successful

---

5 Chris Widener, *Leadership Rules: How to Become a Leader You Want to Be* (CA: A. Wiley Imprint, 2011), 45

husbands, fathers, business men as well as other vocations and professions. The moral of this story is that a person who is success-oriented has strategies that transcend their job descriptions. After Mike reluctantly accepted listening to the coach's advice, strategies were given to him that could be applied to any business endeavor. His protocols were as follows:

1. You get what you expect.

   In other words his players have to toe the line in academics, moral character, attitudes as well as commitment to the team. Logan said, "He holds team leaders accountable for the team's expectations."

2. You get what you model.

   When leaders on the management level in The Department of Education required Speech Therapists to use a newly developed computer program to take attendance and write annual goals the principal and her designees did not understand the intricacies that this transition required. She could not model or monitor the progress and became an annoying, irritant to staff due to her trying to force issues that were impossible. She had no understanding about the incredible time it took to complete the attendance or errors that had to be rectified before finalization of the work. Additionally we were not given laptops but instead the principal insisted that we could use the new apple computers that were in the computer lab. She did not know that the new computer program was not standardized on the Apple computers in the lab. These computers could only process individual cases and the speech pathologist mainly instructs children in groups of threes and sometimes more. She had no conception of the terrible computer glitch the therapists experienced. Due to not having any models we struggled trying to complete work on a computer that could not organize groups. Not wanting to appear that we no longer could perform our jobs many of us did the work at home on our personal laptops and PC computers. Hours into the night many worked in order to finish the mandated work. The bottom line to this historical commentary is the United Federation of Teachers Union got involved and a lawsuit was filed. The union won and every speech therapist received a very large extra check. There was not any one to model the new demanding work required to perform our assigned duties or to give the proper equipment. Managers must be good models for employees to do work efficiently within the time frame that is legally allowed with adequate tools or equipment.

3. You get what you reward.

   The management of our timeshare promised my husband and me, "If we get a few people to come to the Poconos and watch a ninety minute presentation that we would get an eighty dollar dinner certificate in a restaurant there. They added if any one bought a timeshare, we would get not only dinner but a free massage or manicure. Well we made sure we invited people that qualified according to their income requirement. One bought as well as others visited so we scored twice! If we were not enticed by the rewards promised we would not have tried half as hard! What tasty and relaxing rewards. Both management and the consumer benefited from this reward system.

Persistence

Persistence is an element in a leader that says I will never give up. It may be considered to some a do or die philosophy. When many say it cannot be done, a persistent leader will say the battle has just begun. My expressing facts poetically will drill into one's mind the winning stance that a determined leader embraces. Not many thought that Nelson Mandela could run a country that just came out of Apartheid without horrific bloodshed. He surprised many by persistently showing love to Caucasians, as well as insisting on a United South Africa for all ethnic groups. A wonderful Book was written by Mandela that graphically displayed great opposition to his nonviolent methodology but he would not flinch (*Long Walk to Freedom: The Autobiography of Nelson Mandela 1995).*[6] A movie was made in 2009 about his life called *Invictus*. The meaning of Invictus in Latin means undefeated or unconquerable. Invictus was the name of Mandela's favorite poem written by an English poet named William Ernest Henley. Presentation of Henley's poem here evidences the reason why after twenty–seven years of incarceration Mandela remained sane as well as optimistic.

---

6 Nelson Mandela, *Long Walk to Freedom: The Autobiography of Nelson Mandela* (New York: Little Brown and Co., 1995) 379

Invictus

Out of the night that covers me,
Black as the pit from pole to pole,
I thank whatever gods may be
For my unconquerable soul.

In the fell clutch of circumstance
I have not winced nor cried aloud.
Under the bludgeoning of chance
My head is bloody, but unbowed.

Beyond this place of wrath and tears
Looms but the horror of the shade,
And yet the menace of the years
Finds, and shall find, me unafraid.

It matters not how strait the gate,
How charged with punishments the scroll,
I am the master of my fate,
I am the captain of my soul.

Mandela was so motivated to succeed that diligence was his only option. Due to his determination that South Africa would be united at all cost he was internationally admired and recognized. In 1993, Mandela shared the Nobel Prize for Peace, with Frederik Willem de Klerk (the previous leader of South Africa) for the successful termination of the Apartheid regime and laying the foundation for a democratic government in South Africa. Mandela was a model of persistence for all humanity.

CHAPTER II

Dispositions that Affect Leaders and Followers

A. Followers' Attitudes that Impact Leaders

There are attitudes or virtual stances that leaders take that can prosper them or limit or cause their business to fail. These attitudes affect both men and women. Depending on what the leader's skeleton is in the closet it may affect both genders the same or women and men may differ percentile wise in loss or gain. Some corporations have sensitive leaders, which have daycare facilities to aid female workers that have infants and still need or desire to work. Wonderful! Stress is released off these women. The running to a home or nursery a distance away with a baby is tiring and a cause of frustration and sometimes anxiety. When women are tired or worried about their child while on the job, their creativity or work output is affected. When a child is close to the mother she may at times be able to check on the child on her lunch hour or during breaks. Corporations or hospitals that can afford and have a giving attitude to assist struggling women with a daycare will have a payoff in less lateness and absenteeism of female staff or managers depending on their position. Since I successfully raised a child as a single parent I know firsthand the pressure that would have been alleviated but that was not in the era that my child was raised. I would have been overjoyed if on the job or school daycares were an option. Instead I suffered from tiredness and worry about my child.

Managers with the wrong attitudes feel it is not necessary to explain to team members why a decision was made that affects staff could cause dissention (Travis Bradberry and Jean Greaves).[7] Lack of knowledge of rationale has an effect on their morale. The sharing of information through meetings or discussions creates feelings of inclusion instead of personnel just going through the mechanics of a job. There are times though when it is not appropriate to tell staff or team members why changes are being made on a job. What comes to my mind is the owner of the establishment may be taking a risk that may affect the security of one or more jobs. If successful he may have to hire more but if unsuccessful he may have to downsize. Also there may be some necessary staff members that are too critical, making it best to wait on outcomes rather than being bothered by negative undermining remarks or assertions.

---

7 Travis Bradberry and Jean Greaves, *Leadership 2* (San Diego: Talent Smart, 2012) 190

Followers lack respect for leaders they do not like. So when a change is implemented by the leader the follower due to their negative feelings are not capable of looking at the change objectively. In other words they may complain or be personally angered by it because of a judgmental view exhibited because of their poor relationship with the leader. Maxwell stated in his book, "People tend to view change like they view the change agent." This consequence demonstrates that it is important for leaders to work on being liked by as many staff, team member, auxiliary members or employees as possible. No leader wants to deal with unnecessary friction about a beneficial change on a job.

Other character features rise up in the work place when changes are implemented. If the follower does not have an open mind even though he may like the leader he may shut down if any change in the way of doing things occurs. A person's home behavior is sometimes affected by new occurrences on the job. Some wives accuse their husbands of not being able to move on or change. On the job he may be among the few who are complaining about a change. "The old way was just fine with me." He may believe in that old adage, "if it ain't broke why fix it." Others who desire to move on with the new way may perceive that he has a narrow mind or consider him backward.

B. Outcomes Resulting From Various Negative Attitudes of Leaders

Leaders themselves sometimes are resistant to change if they themselves developed a program that is now being phased out by their up line (Maxell). Even though they are leaders themselves they may not be capable of seeing the change objectively. This is the reason why managers, principals, auxiliary heads, club and team leaders need to study by reading books on leadership. Perhaps even meetings should be set up to turn key (to pass on information) what they learned in order to stop tensions and sometimes unnecessary disruptions in the workplace. They in this manner can amend some erred thinking. After all everyone desires to be happy and not angered by distorted, twisted surmising that can even terminate with loss of position or employment.

In the time that we live in most people desire a lot of leisure time. If a leader implements a change on a job that requires more investment of time many may reject it. Even if there is an additional benefit or money time may be preferred. If there is a union on the job time allotment may be filed as an issue for discussion with managers, CEO's and other heads of departments. An unwanted fight for time with or without pay may ensue. On a job that is not unionized the time consuming change may be forced through but in the long run a loss of some workers may occur as they find new employment.

CHAPTER III

Leadership Theories as Well as Reasons for Usage

A. What Drives Various Theory Usage

Organizational Leadership in general consists of men and women who are leaders who have the capability of running businesses, agencies, churches, schools, clubs, or programs. These leaders' duties include facilitation of changes of staffs' behavior through motivation and direction of employees or the organization's members. These leaders very often have to elicit professional advice from consulting firms that contract out experts to organizations (Jane Hyun and Audrey S. Lee's book, *Flex the New Playbook for Managing across Differences*). Basically organizational leaders work for private, public or nonprofit businesses. They excel in human resource management, employee development, employee compensation, as well as employee recruitment. Organizational leaders also work as corporate trainers, lecturers, motivational speakers, program developers, as well as in instructional design. They also take on various administrative roles in schools, colleges, and agencies. Of course leadership in the field of information technology can never be overlooked. Additionally leaders often head research projects, are accountants, finance experts, family firm leaders, as well as church managerial leaders.

The purpose of the increase in managerial organization leadership today is due to the knowledge that strong leaders reduce operating cost for the establishments that they work permanently for or do consultations. Because our nation is currently trying to come out of a recession, businesses have to run with very limited funds. The department of Education which I worked for is a good example of an establishment that suffered huge budget cuts. The need for strategic motivational leadership to keep the biggest hirer in the city afloat was mandatory. There is currently an ever present awareness that contented employees will stay working for a business as well as demonstrate more productivity than disgruntled workers.

B. Leadership Theory Examples

Today's theories of leadership have a tendency not to stress character traits per se. It was imperative to give the information on personality traits so that the new ideas are conceptualized from the fundamental base in which it grew an offshoot. Nowadays a relational study is made between the leader and the follower and workable plans or policies are formed that will benefit the business. An example of a modern theory employed today would be concentration on leadership styles that focus on a variety of situations instead of the traits of the leader.[8] The thinking used to be that leaders had to be born. The new concentration is on how to impact the life of a follower (worker) to the extent that he is more of an asset to a firm or business. This in my thinking is a design shift because the leader is now being manipulated by the employees. I can imagine the conversation between the manager and his staff. Perhaps it world go like this: The manager tells the staff whatever way you want to do the job today will be acceptable. Just do the best you can. After the worker completes the job he will be asked what was good and what could be improved in his (the employee) estimation. Next the manager will give suggestions to aid him in ameliorating what he himself said was his weakness. Seems to me that now the firm is employee driven and the managers adapt to the employees. Feedback has been used to find out what makes a worker a success or failure. The worker's successes have now changed the manager's thinking and as an adjunct improved his managerial skills. The worker, in return has improved morale due to success in using his own methodology.

Of course any changes in any field of endeavor are usual accomplished by new nomenclature evidencing a broader or different scope or territory. Well here are two of the twentieth century "theory words" pertaining to leadership; "situational" and "transformational" leadership. Well I am

8 Ken Blanchard, Patricia Zigarmi and Drea Zigarmi, *Leadership and the One Minute Manager: Increasing Effectiveness Through Situational Leadership* (NYC: Harper Books, 2013), 54-56

glad I got that out! In Ken Blanchard, Patricia Zigarmi and Drea Zigami's book there is an interesting chapter called, "*Different Strokes for Different Folks.*" This section of the book really is saying, 'A leader sometimes must adapt his style to the specific situations or traits of the workers.' The explanatory examples given that clarify the above statement will now be provided. "A strong totalitarian leader is a good choice for unskilled workers." He has a domineering personality. In other words it is either his way or hit the highway. "A democratic style leader works best with creative and highly skilled workers." The manager may ask for a vote on which material is best for them to do the work, with the type of tools given or the time frame they have for completion of the work. The way to memorize the above leadership styles is to think of it as a match game. Situational leaders have the capability of changing according to the needs of the workers as was shown in my example above. They are adaptable people. You can feel the strong impact of the word adaptable if you think of the transition a person has to make that has spent his or her entire childhood in a tropical country and then moves to Alaska. The first thing the person will buy is several hooded fur lined jackets as well as fur lined boots and gloves. If you look at a before and after picture of them they will not be recognizable because the situation warranted a drastic change in order for the individual to survive. The same struggle on an intellectual level takes place in businesses, schools, clubs, programs and teams. The difference is it is not only a fight to survive but additionally the combat is for the main purposes of the entity to be achieved as well as a profit. Some of the purposes of these establishments may be to alleviate suffering if it is health facilities; financing housing developments for middle income if it is a realtor; providing entertainment for teenagers if it is a recreational facility in addition to many other descriptions for other establishments. The desire is for the commitment for every endeavor to be optimally achieved. In other words much more than financial survival of various entities have to be examined in order to be considered to have the desired results!

C. The Style that Transforms Through Goal Facilitation

No, the transformational type of leader was not forgotten. The meaning of this type of leadership I will simplify. They are motivational leaders of employees, club members or members of any type of purposeful team or program. From an article, written by a woman's organization I belong to the following was learned: *The Advantages of Emerging Leadership Theories*, Kechner and Media's thesis is, "transformational leaders model the mannerisms, ideas and standards they desire their protégés to achieve. They achieve this by using a goal facilitation plan." Transformational leadership is really a subdivision of all the other leadership styles. Getting necessary understandings of one leadership style was imperative before adding the motivational piece. This excelling element gets the various styles moving in a positive direction with results. In other words successful businesses, clubs programs, or teams obviously had transformational leadership in order to have gotten to their fruitful end. It feels to me like the yeah, yeah, team effort when one goes to a game. Transformational leaders cheer their workers on in overt or covert ways in order to facilitate individuals or groups of workers to do their best.

This book is detailing situational leadership. In Debbie Silverman and Trish Carr's book, *It's Just a Conversation*, it was noted that on jobs, 10% of people are low performers, 70% want to do a good job and are trainable, and 20% of workers are top performers.[9] An example of what would happen if a manager is not functioning in the situational leadership style will be given first. "Chris we are a week away from the deadline and I haven't received your outlines." 'Sorry boss, I'm working on it. I got backed up because...' Boss: "I don't need excuses if I don't have it on my desk before five you're off the team." Situation managers are trained to show their staff, team or club members that they have value by not interrupting them and placing incredible pressure on them. If the boss had allowed the team leader to finish he may have discovered that he was delayed because he was waiting for some figures to come in from accounting before detailing the outline. He would have promised to give him it right after he received the final statistics. This boss was judgmental and was not capable of keeping the relationship with the team member whole. Instead he could have taken on a coaching stance and asked him to let him know if the Accounting Department is detaining him from handing in his work in a timely fashion. In this manner Chris would have apologized for the lack of communication and the boss would kept a highly motivated member of the team.

In the book, *Leading with Purpose and Clarity* by Joanna Barsh and Johanne Lavoie two styles of management are

---

9 Debbie Silverman and Trish Carr, *It's Just a Conversation: What to Say and How to Say It in Business* (ParkerHouse Books 2014) 15

explained demonstrating the need for knowledge of both types.[10] It is also appropriate to mention here that a mixture of both leadership styles can be implemented by the same leader when appropriate. Coaching that should have been used in the beginning of the scenario with Chris and his boss is usage of the supportive methodology. The other type which is not exemplified here is called directive. The supportive style of management is used with staffs or teams that demonstrate a desire to learn. The uses of mentors or sponsors are really functioning support managers that are situation based. Their interest is to propel leaders into a level of outstanding performance instead of fair to mediocre. Thus mentorship and sponsorship positions are really advocators of managers by being, motivational facilitators.

---

10 Joanna Barsh and Johanne Lavoie, *Centered Leadership: Leading with Purpose* (New York: Crown Publishing 2014) 156-167

CHAPTER IV

Highlighted Differences Between Family Led Businesses and Other Firms

A. Problems Family Businesses Face

The reason I chose to do a simple comparison analysis between family firms and other types of businesses is my desire for readers to decode new possibilities or upgrades of their ideas. Actual transformation of ideas can be formulated for those who have starter businesses or firms. Without delving into the business text books that I have perused, there are extremely important examples of the differences that privately owned family firms exhibit. The term private demonstrates some exclusion of others. There is a difference if one says, 'This is my business,' than if someone says, 'our corporation.'

Exclusion of participation from owners of family firms from obedience to certain rules or laws will differ with the type of firm and what controls or restraints are implemented for them to follow. The United States government has now through the vote of Supreme Court Justices and some politicians passed laws that have redefined marriage. It is now extended to same sex couples (Marriage Equality Act). Additionally an extension to legalized abortions has been passed that allows a morning after pill (Plan B Contraceptive).These laws have impacted various family businesses because their religious beliefs are oppositional to what these laws demand. The Affordable Health Care Act (2013) was the vehicle that caused interference in the normal flow of some of their firms. It contains a requirement for the leaders of these family firms to pay for their employee's use of plan B contraceptives which induces abortion at the very onset of conception. It is against various religious values to pay for their employees to abort a zygote or fetus. Also some religions are against same sex marriage. There has been a lawsuit against a family-owned bakery that refused to bake a wedding cake for a homosexual couple. So you see there can be a large gulf between the functioning of family and other businesses because of their personal value component. Family businesses have much more personal dealing with their workforce than other businesses. Owners that hold to their values have been having sleepless nights. Many times they were forced to hire lawyers to fight an onslaught of court cases while other businesses and big corporations peacefully went along with these laws. For many, these laws are immoral. Fortunately, for the cake-maker in May 2018, he finally won the case and is able to relax because he is not going against his religious beliefs. Unfortunately, the case was only for his specific business and other businesses still have to individually continue to fight for their religious beliefs not to be overridden by a government law causing the termination of their business. Presently modification of the law that forces family businesses to pay for prescriptions for plan B and other types of contraception that are oppositional to their believes are being modified. What a cost to family firms that opposed this bill stress-wise as well as for some financial loses.

In other businesses there are also employees and possibly even one of the owners, board members or stock holders that also disagree or are opposed to nontraditional marriage and are not pro-choice but they are forced to cooperate with the legal status quo. It is known that the rule on most of these jobs is, "Do not talk about religion or politics!" Instead of an interruptive court fight it is business as usual. The undercurrent of complaints never comes to the forefront in these businesses to be addressed. I used to be employed by the Department of Education of the City of New York. It is the biggest hirer in the City. No one is outwardly voicing their opinion about abortion or gay marriage in any productive manner. Just hush, hush talk among colleagues behind closed doors. A lesbian teacher had a baby by artificial insemination. The proud picture of her with her homosexual partner was posted by the clock for all staff to scan. No remarks were made except "What a beautiful baby." There definitely was a powerful undercurrent that never came to the forefront. So it was business as usual in the school building. All of the above going on would be disallowed in many family businesses which believe only in the traditional female and male union in marriage. What dissimilarity between many family firms and huge government conglomerates!

B. Analysis of Family Businesses Versus Other Businesses

There are various other differences between family firms and other businesses. What comes to my mind is that sibling rivalry can raise its ugly head in family businesses. Two twins ran a speech, occupational and physical therapy contracting agency and when they had a meeting for the entire therapeutic staff one twin constantly interrupted the other. This interruptive behavior took place when it was time to train us about the intricacies of her expertise which was speech and language pathology. The interrupter, her sister was an occupational and physical therapist and headed that department. I was present when one of the twins that was interrupted gave the reason why. "It must be understood that we're twins." The other sister then responded, "well I am sorry about that." Of course this kind of problem is unique to family businesses.

A fight over the control of a family business can also occur if the parent or head of the business dies or is too sick to function (Jane Hilbert).[11] Other businesses and corporations often have an assistant in place that can take over if necessary. Older family leaders often refuse to allude

[11] Jane Hilbert-Davis, W. Gibb Dyer, Jr., *Consulting to Family Businesses: A Practical Guide to Contracting, Assessment, and Implementation* (San Francisco, Pfeiffer a Wiley Imprint) 24

to the fact that they cannot live forever. Thus there is no plan for take over due to stubbornness. Also at times they may allow a family member to still work while they have an apparent severe disability that causes loss of customers. I remember needing an eye exam and new glasses. The owner allowed his very elderly mother who had constant facial involuntary muscle movements to test eyes. Even though I am a speech and language pathologist and work with handicapped persons I was in need of a service myself at that time and was not in an understanding mode. It was obvious that nepotism was the reason she was still working. Although, I allowed her to take care of me I never went back to that establishment. It is just that one desires to be relaxed when in need of personal service. Her condition was unnerving especially for numerous persons who are not sensitive to the needs of handicapped persons. Employees that have problems in other businesses are governed by rules that will force very ill persons to go on disability or retire if he or she are above a certain age. Even unionized jobs like the Department of Education will not allow people that have illnesses that deter them from their job description to continue to work. The employees are cognizant of the fact that they have no recourse if they cannot adequately perform their duties. Flashing back to a time my car got hit by a garbage truck and I received nerve damage, The Department of Education documented that I could not return to work for 1 year. Even though I was able to work in six months, I was forced to follow their guidelines!

Some Family Businesses are not only headed by a family member but all of the upper echelons also are family members. Other family businesses have some key people that are not family members such as managers or team leaders. Unlike non-family businesses, non-family managers in family businesses have double trouble. Non-family managers have to establish a good rapport with family members as well as do a good job. Sometimes family executives may leave the non-family manager out of important business plans or discussions. This often occurs because the family members have different values from the outsider. It is my understanding that this could be viewed as undermining an equal professional. What I see also is when there is an opportunity for upward mobility sometimes a relative may be elevated when the outsider is more suited or competent for the position. Of course other types of corporations do not have these types of problems.

Business dealings are also altered at times due to a non-family manager hired as mentors to younger family business members. These managers sometimes will limit negative comments or feedback to these young people due to the inherent risk to his or her managerial position. I found it interesting to know that their inhibiting feedback helps to create developmental handicaps for the next generation of leaders. I view this negative occurrence as being likened to young people believing a lie and passing it on to their children!

C. Assistance that will Anchor Family Businesses into a Success Mode

The good happening that is being spread presently is the use of family-business consultants. “They are capable of capturing the whole gestalt of their business and work with non-family, and family managers as well as outside advisors."[12] Using what I call correlating measures the consultant is able to help a family business to formulate plans that grow the business as well as help keep family unity. The consultant actually does a comparison analysis with other businesses that are not managed or owned by a family member. Usage of match up charts between the two kinds of businesses boldly demonstrates differences and failures due to some of the differences in both family firms and other businesses. Venn diagrams which are really a system of interlocking circles also causes aspects of the successes and failures of the two types of businesses to be blatantly highlighted. Venn diagrams are even better than matching charting at times because you can easily see what is similar about the two businesses by reading the writing in the center of the interlocking circles. Statistical presentations of the successes in other businesses given by non-family impartial experts many times can take the wind out of the sails of stubborn inflexible family members.

In my estimation consultants for family led businesses most possibly advise others by using contingency. It probably sounds like this, 'If you (an elderly or physically ill owner) vote on who can succeed you in six months to a year and train him or her you will be almost guaranteed your business assets will not continue to plummet. You can stay on as a part-time advisor afterwards.' Many more efforts to align themselves with successful non-family businesses will begin to occur after consultations with striking statistics of other business successes are shown and discussed!

---

12 Jane Hilbert-Davis, W. Gibb Dyer, Jr., *Consulting to Family Businesses: A Practical Guide to Contracting, Assessment, and Implementation* (San Francisco, Pfeiffer a Wiley Imprint) 100

CHAPTER V

Communication Expertise for Leaders

A. Mechanics of Speech

The actual manner in which one pronounces words has a great impact on a leader's audience. There are some brilliant people who are inarticulate. As a speech pathologist I have noticed a reaction and voiced complaints from various types of listeners. Some are unforgiving and others have the loving understanding that there is not anyone who is perfect. One type of person that is the most intolerant is a person that is usually status conscious whether they are wealthy or keeping up a front struggling. Others that have Master's or Doctorate degrees may be unduly stuck on a speaker's production of speech instead of above average content. Since the leader is cognizant of his shortcoming what I have personally seen helped is an open admittance that he knows he or she mispronounces words at times. "Just listen and you will gain from what is being said. After all I am giving directions and information about important changes that are being made that will affect you." Many people can relax after that and distraction is then minimized. Of course if a leader has a more serious impairment it is best for them to use a designee to speak on their behalf.

B. Basic Language Usage and Dialectical Differences and their Acceptance

Leaders that speak grammatically incorrect also have a problem that may or may not be severe. Others, who speak culturally different non-standard dialects of English sometimes, additionally may not be tolerated. It depends on what type of business, club or team they are leading. Scholarly English in the United States is White Anglo-Saxon Standard English based. In an academic setting varied dialects or individuals that speak grammatically incorrect are mostly not tolerated. In order to be successful one may have to take a course to ameliorate grammatical errors for poor speakers of English. Those who speak a culturally different dialect many times must learn how to code switch and approximate a more standard version of English, before continuing up the ladder of success in an administrative or managerial position. Clubs may not have such problems. For confidence sake or for financial increase it is best to either pay a teacher or speech therapist or take courses to improve. Certain individuals whom you want to impress may believe that a person in leadership should be able to communicate on a higher level in order to deal adequately with the public. Temporarily one can confess awareness that they are not speaking correct grammatical English. He or she could possibly continue by saying, 'it is important that these details are received no matter what!' Reiterate, 'You need to receive this message.' Although, this will diminish listener's distraction the leader should desire to work on improvement if in error or code switch if another dialect is spoken.

In general leaders all have to put their use of speech and language deliberately on a conscious level at times. If the aim is to change certain aspects of your language usage concentration is a necessity. Your speaking must be placed on a conscious level due to the fact that speech is perishable. Words that exit your month's vibrations, immediately are carried by the air into the listener's ear and are gone. A business in this manner can be an instant success or an instant flop. So if the objective of a business is to effect change in personnel that will take a business, church, team, school, or audience of consumers or patriots in another direction, enhancement of language usage has to be managed. Facilitation of these changes is not easy because people many times are content with the manner in which they speak and are resistant to change. Others desire to change but do not want the hours of work that it takes to change something about them that feels natural. Leaders have to understand the emotional components of individuals in order to be successful in motivating them to alter their behavior and achieve corrective or Standard English speech and language goals.

C. Necessity of Interpretation of Your Downlines, or Employees' Emotions

Managers and team leaders must be mood detectors. If managers know staff or team members well, if extreme unhappiness is exhibited by any of them, it should be identified even though the person did not voice a problem. Speech pathologists call this speech reading. It does not only include reading lips which is not necessary when people are speaking audibly. What speech reading deals with other than this is observation of facial expressions, eye movement, contact or lack of, posture, positioning of the body as well as gestures. If someone you know becomes nervous or tense after the mention of something important it is many times noticeable.

In businesses that require consultations with others, motivational speaking, trainings or workshops, the speakers must make and maintain good eye contact. In the book, *It's Just a Conversation*, the salient points brought out about eye contact is as follows:

a. Successful business people make and maintain eye contact 50% to 60% of the time.

b. If the speakers eyes have a glazed look it represents boredom.

c. If a speaker has direct eye contact it means honesty.

d. If a speaker has two little eye contact it could mean lying, or being impolite.

e. The natural way to maintain eye contact is to look away occasionally for a couple of seconds as you listen then return eye contact.

In the book *Leadership 2*, a job scenario was given. On this job speech reading is considered connecting emotionally with people. In other words the manager reacts supportive when body language deems necessary. If things are moving along he complements. In a specific situation on a job, a manager noticed everyone did not appear to be fully engaged in a team project. He observed which personnel were making the most progress toward finishing the project. Next, he announced the project focus had changed from its original plan. In doing so the ones that were unsuccessful in moving the project along were able to bow out without being offended. Now the competent workers were not hindered by re-explaining what needed to be accomplished over and over or having to terminate unworkable ideas. The project was completed by the most knowledgeable!

A national example of a debate that the public judged heavily by posture, voice volume, pitch, emphasis and facial expression (speech reading) was the last presidential debate between President Barack Obama and his Republican opponent Mitt Romney in 2012. Personally, I viewed this as an almost total disaster. The high rating towards Obama getting a second term in office dropped tremendously. Obama seemed to have a dry, listless, hesitant, tone of voice as well as a carriage that showed uncertainty. Romney seemed to address the audiences with a loud exciting, competent, voice volume. Romney disciplined himself to radiate youthful, alertness, and exuberance even though he is an older man. His active bouncy type of stance seemed to make him appear to be more up with national and international events. Many thought Romney would win after that debate. The then candidate for vice president Biden was able to bring Obama's rating back up with his performance during the debate with his opponent Paul Ryan. During the debate the much younger candidate made a very serious remark that seemed to take the intended effect on the audience. Immediately Biden threw his head back and had a hardy youthful ho, ho, ho which was extremely unusual for a much older matured man who had signs of balding. This absurd laughter had the effect of making the younger candidate appear to be too immature, and inexperienced to be a viable candidate. A Velma Osborne hypothesis can be made here. 'No matter how much of a genius you are if you are not able to come out of your own personality at times to make a point by acting out sentences or phrases, you will lose some followers.'

D. General Understanding of Defense Mechanism can be Fruitful

If someone becomes verbally defensive or offensive, speech is a psychological process. What could be done is informally diagnose the problem. Reading a simplified book on Defense Mechanisms can give you a heads up on why individuals project certain irritating behaviors at times. Anna Freud's more complicated book, *The Ego and the Mechanism of Defense* can be perused after a study of a more simplified book of your chose.[13] In general people do things at times to protect themselves (defense mechanisms). If understood, a manager will not desire to immediately fire or demote someone if there is a change on the job and the

---

13 Ann Freud, *The Ego and the Mechanism of Defense* (London, Kornac Books 1966) 59

individual becomes offensive. It just might be a fear of how they can continue to fit in there. If defense mechanisms are understood, a manager may feel it's worth the wait or additional explanations of how the employee can adapt to the changed environment or position.

E. Simile, Metaphor and Use of Linguistic Ploys Draw Interest

Usage of similes, metaphors and cultural references are power rhetorical devises to pick up the interest of others (Jill Geiser).[14] I remember when I was growing up a radio disc-jockey would come on the air exclaiming, "I'm your Wolf Man Jack." Since he was not seen many people thought he was African American. When featured on a television program the irony was revealed. He was a Caucasian using a metaphor with cultural ties to the Black Community. The saying means to a Black person that he is tough or strong which is a characteristic many African men have taken on due to negativity in the ghetto environment. It is a survival mode or defense mechanism. Using this colloquial expression Wolf Man was thought to be "cool." His use of a metaphor with cultural connotation was very successful. He was one of the well-known lead disc jockeys out of many at that time.

Similes are great for making a simple analysis. A simile that comes to my mind that is extremely effective is taken from the Bible. Here is a paraphrase. God will make your sins white as snow (Isaiah 1:18). As you know sin has nothing to

---

14 Jill Geiser, *Work Happy: What Great Bosses Know* (NYC: Center Street: Hachette Book Group, 2012) 29

do with color but instead distasteful or harmful acts or evil or filthy communication. This well-known sentence means that God can put those who believe in his existence through a purification process. In other words you will not do acts contrary to law or use filthy communication any longer if you submit your heart to God. God wipes your slate clean and you now function as if you are a new person. This is a picturesque way to draw attention to erred ways that many times lead to failure in one's personal life as well as business ventures.

Business leaders can reach staff at meetings by using linguistic ploys that hold the listeners attention. Use of parallelism is one of the ways. Parallelism is the use of synonyms to the extent that the second line in a message repeats itself. Antithetic parallelism means the use of an opposing idea within one sentence. An example would be as follows: Sales persons that keep a smile on their faces will make many sales but those that are fretful will fail. Synthetic parallelism is a good method to get staff or club members to remember or better yet embrace a behavior that will aid them in making a change in their behaviors. The same thought is repeated in the same sentence. Looking back at a sales seminar I attended numerous years ago I still remember what a leading salesperson said. "We all hold up a shield, a façade and say well you can't come in." Being a quiet person I understood exactly what he was sharing with us. He was using synthetic parallelism to say people have to open up more and come out of their personalities in order to be successful in sales. It did impress me enough to be a little more open with people at that time.

Use of hyperbole can make the meaning of a statement last due to its emphatic value. It is an exaggeration of a truth to the extent that it may be quite humorous. I heard a comedian say that she had so much plastic surgery that she was recommended for recycling! Although plastic surgeons will not like that remark, those that are overzealous to make severe or continual changes in themselves may think twice about it before continuing on a self-destructive path.

F. Educational Rap or Use of Poetic Language Assists in Learning Skills

Language used in a rhythmic manner in unexpected scenarios by leaders can create interest on a job that never occurred before. A principal allowed an educational rapper to present at a staff development meeting. Never were there such enthusiastic responses to training in an academic forum. My colleagues became inundated with ideas facilitated by the unique bombardment of verbal rhythm. He had grammatical raps, science raps and social studies raps. Most other staff development sessions are ho hum and very few teachers implement what they learned or the redundant information that they already knew. Teachers as well as Speech Therapist observed that children that had trouble memorizing or understanding the meaning of science or social studies words now had a vehicle to learn. Children that speak non-standard versions of English were able to write in Standard English which is necessary in order to become scholarly. The grammatical raps showed the mismatch between the Standard English and Black dialects of English. Additionally, I personally walked into a classroom where I took out a few children for speech therapy and heard and saw a Sight Word Rap on a screen in front of a bouncing kindergarten class. What a fun way beginning readers were being engaged to learn. Even the slowest child will get some musical clues in not only how to read but spell the words also! What a motivational innovative learning tool was being used with great results. Since interpretation of music or rhythm is on the right side of the brain and speech and language is on the left side of the brain children who had mild to moderate speech and language deficiencies or impairments were able to learn information that they were not able to learn or memorize before. Adding rhythm to the syllabus went over big with wonderful results!

Christian Rap was also introduced into some churches by Clergy and Pastors. The good thing that came out of it is some church leaders were able to get the interest, sometimes of young people who may have had bad breaks in life and were incompletely socialized. Delinquents, abused, economically depraved, those disenfranchised due to racial stigmas or children from dysfunctional or foster families need specialized assistance. Many that would have become lost in the streets or incarcerated now were functioning well in certain church programs or services. The leaders understood that a bridge needed to be used to bring some youth into the morality upheld in the word of God. Christian rap was at least helping in bridging the gap temporarily until the anointed Word of God opportunistically grabbed a hold of them.

G. Networking Knowledge Promotes Continuation of Business or Social Dealings

It was discovered that networking belongs in this language usage section due to its sole dependence on the vocal. In the book, *It's Just a Conversation*, five important points to do effective networking were brought out.[15]

- Make it a conversation not a monologue.
- Sound authentic.
- Stay attentive.
- Talk to and about them.
- Stay on point, be succinct.

Immediate failures occur when a networker hands a business card to someone who only says "What do you do?" I call these "file thirteen" cards. In other words you do not even remember who or what so you throw them out. Giving out cards with no dialogue may mean to the receiver you are unsure of yourself or lack good speech and language skills.

Networking requires planning. You have to know how many people you want to meet and have the time to both listen and speak to them. Also you have to give them a good idea about what you desire. You may have to plan to come out of your comfort zone and act differently then you normally do. Personally, I would wear a bright color but a very conservative styled outfit in order to stand out in a good way. I would be like sunshine. So in that way I would be approachable.

Here are a few more tips from Rebecca Shambaugh's book *Make Room For Her*, on being successful at networking. You have to introduce yourself with both your first and

---

15 Jill Geiser, *Work Happy: What Great Bosses Know* (NYC: Center Street: Hachette Book Group, 2012) 29, 40

last names and allow them to do most of the talking. Additionally, you must ask open ended questions, connect them with other people, be interested, not interesting, listen attentively, nod, react, and find common ground. Showing common ground is of the most importance because at first the person you are interacting with may not see any apparent need to create a relationship with you.

One day I exchanged cards with someone that at first I thought may not be mutually beneficial. After I listened to her for a while she explained to me that her organization was against Violence to woman. Since I am a pastoral mentor I thought well maybe I could be of some assistance in the future. I knew this would be on a volunteer basis. When I told her I was an author of a book, she inquired about the title. I told her it was entitled, *Autobiography of Velma Osborne: Reflects on African American History*. She immediately said she would buy the book and read it. After reading it she gave me compliments and to my surprise asked me to be a speaker at her organization's Black History Program, whose main speaker was from the Mayor's Office's Unit to Combat Domestic Violence. Well the wheels began turning in my head. As a successful person who was raised in Harlem I had a lot to offer. The bottom line is part of my success was being published so that could be announced at their affair. The book is a motivational, informative tool and that is why she asked me to speak. I am going to add one more important point to networking. 'You must have patience.'

CHAPTER VI

AUDIENCES TARGETED AND OUTCOMES

A. Group Types

THERE ARE MANY TYPES of groups that various, managers, motivational speakers, union leaders or faith based leaders have to deal with. It would be impossible for me to touch bases with all. I will expose aspects of a few. In other words I will be putting a dent in a maze so that if you choose you could branch out in all directions. Jane Hyun, and Audrey S. Lee gave me a start in their book *Flex the New Playbook for Managers*, by studying their glossary of Key Terms.[16] They had a term called, "Four Generations in the Work Place."

16 Jane Hyun, and Audrey S. Lee, *Flex the New Playbook for Managing Across Differences* (New York: Harper Collins 2014) xxvi

Yes, this term jumped out at me. There was also interesting sub-headings that gave me the full understanding of the necessity for a descriptive breakdown of each of the four divisions. It sent me down memory lane of how my grandparents, parents and aunts and uncles spoke about the generations before theirs. The impression I received from my parents was that their parents were stricter and much more inflexible. Perfection at all cost may have been their motto. It is useful to focus on the term, "Four Generations in the Workplace," so that young, middle-aged and senior citizens in business could benefit as to how each changed their focus or ideology and require different means to access their market or sell them on ideas or goods.

The titles of the four groups are as follows: Traditionalist, Baby Boomers, Generation X and Generation Y-Millennials. Paraphrases of the characteristics of each group as well as my additions are necessary so that individual businesses can visualize which group will benefit from their service, club, school or product. In other words very few baby strollers will be sold in a senior citizen community. So a study of the needs of these groups as well as strategic areas where many of them may live in close proximity is needed. Learning about demographics in high school and college was not a waste of time after all. Marketing majors thrive on demographic statistics.

Traditionalists were born before nineteen forty-six. These are people who grew up during the Great Depression and also went through World War II. Responsibility is their motto in addition to respect for authority figures. Looking back I remember my father telling us how he worked hard in a vegetable market making an incredible low salary that was sacrificially shared with his younger siblings because his mother died when he was sixteen. He exhibited a responsibility that today is very rarely seen.

Baby boomers were born from nineteen forty-six to nineteen sixty-four. Individualism was emphasized during this time. The extended family started to decrease and nuclear families began to increase. Young people today consider baby boomers to be naïve. Even though most were naïve they worked hard and stayed together as a family unit inclusive of grandparents and sometimes aunts and uncles. They were optimistic that no matter what they would make it.

Generation X were born between nineteen sixty-five and nineteen seventy-six. These children of the boomers are much more flexible than their parents as well as being more independent. They are much more inclined to analyze things and do not take anything at face value. In the earlier Boomer generation when people watched the news they assumed it was all true. They did not understand that some content was sometimes biased, untrue or exaggerated. Generation X investigates more and knows there are definite reasons why some ideas are promoted on mass media. They figured out many times news events are promoted just to make money or to persuade someone to believe an untruth for someone's selfish purposes.

Generation Y-Millennials were born between nineteen seventy-seven and nineteen ninety-four. I call them computer, iPad and cell phone addicts. Also they are lovers of social media and video games. They do not usually respect hierarchy arrangement of things but instead respect competence versus title. They definitely stress having various outlets but do have a sense of civic duty. The news does bring out a gathering through social media of these young people many times for a worthy cause.

Of course the above generation piece has to be conjoined with gender, culture and ethnicity, when targeting consumers, staff, as well as the higher echelon decision makers. Economic status also has to join the mixture. When dealing with a low income population the products sold must be within their reach (an example would be Dollar Stores and Brand Names for Less Stores). High income populations can deal with exclusive boutiques and designer clothing. Decisions have to be made about what avenue you have to walk down to get to your next plateau and with whom. Truly life is a smorgasbord.

Shambaugh reported in her book that she made a decision to launch a study in 2011 regarding what men thought were the five most beneficial things female executive colleagues had to offer. Rebecca is a sought after speaker for Best Practices for Leading in the Twenty-First Century. She is the founder of Women In Leadership and Learning (WILL) Program which is an executive leadership development program that is focused on research, advancement and retention of women leaders, and executives. A study was undertaken targeting females in order to integrate women positively into segments of the business world, namely executives. The five most appreciated aspects of females learned from men are as follows:

1. How to be a better listener.
2. How to be empathetic.
3. How to think more holistically.
4. How to trust your intuition.
5. How to foster better communication and collaboration.

Shambaugh made the goal to find out what men learned from women in order to hopefully see a more integrated higher echelon in the work force in the future. Statistically speaking eighty percent of executives and Corporate Boards of Directors are male.

The male study also revealed that there is a big change in the workforce now since 2012 when the entrance of millennials occurred. Millennials are different because they saw what happened since 2009 when the United States entered into a recession. They observed people that had twenty to thirty years of service were thrown by the wayside because of the country's failing economy. What this negative scenario created was a need for more women because of the interrogative nature of millennials because of their distrust of businesses. It now takes a higher level of communication to develop supportive relationships with teams. This is because the generations before them were comparatively silent. Today's women have been shown to have more ability to motivate and ameliorate the uncertainties among teams. Scientifically speaking females have the ability to integrate their thoughts using both sides of their brains. This means when there is an onslaught of questions from clients or team members, women have a normal ability to give responses that connect strategic information. Presently some men are becoming very appreciative and comfortable with partnering with female executives. The great disparity between male and female executives is now beginning to diminish.

Sylvia Ann Hewitt in the book, *Top Talent: Keeping Performance Up When Business is Down* also focused on women in managerial positions.[17] Researchers called Catalyst and Mckinsey and Company research evidenced

---

17 Sylvia Ann Hewlett, *Top Talent: Keeping Performance Up When Business is Down* (Boston: Harvard Business Press, 2009) 78-81

that companies that have a number of women in high positions have a much higher return on investments (ROI). Women according to the expert in management Tom Peters, make up eighty three percent of all purchases. It follows that companies that design and sell products in this tight market need women leaders of teams and some team members. Without the right number of women that have the understanding of the needs and desires of other women companies will lose out competition wise.

A European study from a London business school revealed that when work teams had a fifty-fifty divide between men and women the productively went up (Hewlett). This study strongly favors the idea that homogenous groups stubbornly defend wrong ideas because they all basically think alike. Obviously this is a study that uses a deductive methodology. To add to this study a different one that gave statistics serves as a confirmation. Firms in the CAC40 which is the French equivalent to the Dow Jones Industrial Average that had a high percentage of women did better during the financial crisis in a 2008 study. The fewer female managers these businesses had the lower were the prices of their shares of stock. It seems ironic that the more females in high positions leading teams and team members the more insulation there is from going into financial crisis!

It makes sense to target women even though they do not remain in leadership positions as long as their male counterparts. Many times they chose to resign. Women are clingier to family and desire not to work overtime or miss vacations. The focus of women is not as strong as a man to make a lot of money. When efforts are being made to keep female high performers, concessions sometimes have to be presented that are not needed for males. Flexible schedules are a strong draw for many women to want to continue working for a firm. In addition more women than men desire giving back to society. Enticement to get more women may mean showing them how their position is helpful to others. Females also like recognition and may feel hurt and desire to leave if they do not receive it. When firms, corporations or higher education facilities, make allowances for the differences in females' needs then higher retention levels begin to be met.

B. General Ideas for Funding

Funding is actually receipt of a survival strategy for a business. One approach that precedes the usual loan or grants that businesses desire to span them over or start them up is formation of Limited Liability Company (LLC) status. The reason is the business gets tax benefits of a proprietorship or partnership and protection of a corporation shield (Successfully Navigating the Downturns.)[18] It requires getting an identification number (EIN). It is feasible to get an accountant or lawyer to set up LLC's or partnerships because of the onslaught of whistle blowers citing even the slightest infraction of laws. Some infractions are accidently caused. Also ignorance of the law many times is responsible for legal infractions. Manipulations by dishonest predators also cause companies undeserved legal problems.

Some struggling businesses have too much inventory. Too long a time has passed and the expected sales never came. Donald Todrin advised in these cases to liquidate the

---

18 Donald Todrin, *Successfully Navigating The Downturn: Economic and Competitive Survival Strategies* (Madison: Jere Calmes 2011) 54, 138, 139

inventory. It will free capital that can fund the paying of bills that are threating closure of the company. By so doing, a more viable addition to the business can be added that will be more lucrative.

C. Receive Specific Funding Targeted for Charities or Other Businesses

When attending a free Public Library workshop on the usage of media in business, valuable information was given out to the attendees from a representative from The Small Business Administration. The SBA has specialized loans and one targets women entrepreneurs who are considered minorities. These are called, "Growing a Business Loans." It is inclusive of the following aspects that will enhance progress in a business:

- Hiring Employees.
- Employee Benefits.
- Employee Incentives.
- Marketing a Business.
- Exporting.
- Government Contracting.

There was a special offer for women that desired to do business with the government. Woman Owned Small Business (WOSB) Federal Contract Program levels the playing field for women competing for federal contracting opportunities. This particular information can be personalized by making an appointment to speak to one of the SBA representatives.

Other types of financial aid can be given to other specialized groups by the SBA. These groups are namely Green Businesses, Veterans, handicapped, Home-based Businesses, Online Businesses, Franchise Businesses, Self Employed and Independent Contractors, Native Americans and Minority-Owned Businesses. These loans can be used for funding start-up businesses as well as needed expansion or growth of existing businesses.

Ironically while I was reading postings on the New York City subway I saw a sign which targeted minorities, women and others that were called disadvantaged to call and learn about aid for their existing businesses or startups. The MTA advertised on public transportation their Small Business Program which offers assistance in procuring contracts for the already mentioned targeted sector of the population. These contracts would provide work for mass transit or construction projects. It is worth the time of qualified small businesses looking into getting contracts in order to keep their existing employees working or to add more.

You can tell I am not a busy body because I read on another subway train an ad that had a picture of a beaming young woman. She reported that she saved well over seven thousand dollars on Group Health Insurance for her five employees by using a non-profit insurance company called Republic Insurance. A recommendation is made here to check the Better Business Bureau rating on their company before paying for Republic's insurance or any other type. One can also find out if there are other non-profit insurance companies. In any case consultation with other successful businesses as well as the Better Business Bureau is necessary before making any decisions.

Believe this, I was riding on a bus this time and saw a posting that said Business Start-up Opportunities. The web address is startupNY.gov. There was a sub-heading called NYS Empire State Development that is worth investigation because the information highlighted, "ten years tax free for qualified businesses." Keeping profits made without tax liability definitely is a tremendous help. Additionally, a television ad on Startup NY reported if owners decide to have a business in New York the company will not have to pay sales tax either. Furthermore, it was stated that interested start-up leaders or future owners can contact representatives to get assistance and support in moving businesses to New York. Such necessary data as loans and grants can also be procured as well as applications and details about their usage. The more proactive leaders are, the more gathering of funding information from unexpected places will be found.

I received in my mail an advertisement from a firm for small business loans called "On Deck." It boasts about targeting businesses that may have a low credit score. Their theme of persuasion is, "We understand that you cannot judge a business solely on their credit score or their collateral." On Deck examines other decision making data. This firm is interested in checking cash flow when analyzing businesses.

The interest rates for these loans may be higher than banks but funding is fast (sometimes in one day). On Deck also boast of an A plus rating with the Better Business Bureau. They lend to various types of businesses (ex. restaurants, repair shops or retailers) from five thousand to two hundred and fifty thousand dollars.

On Deck loans handle the following:

- Temporary cash flow crunch.
- Increasing staff needs or launching a new marketing campaign.
- A need to buy inventory or equipment.

Applications are given on-line at getondeck.com. One should consult with financial advisors first before trying them.

Formation of certain types of business into a not-for-profit corporation will qualify it to apply for various grants. There are government grants as well as foundational private grants. Receipt of the various types of grants depends on the type of corporation or business venture. Of course a business many times must research how to write a grant or pay a grant writer to be successful in attaining a grant. Once that grant is received the monies must be exactly applied to the staff, products or equipment listed on the given accepted budget flow sheet. Any infractions of the grant guidelines will stop any further dealings with the business and could possibly lead to fines or arrest.

Not-for-profit businesses can also do actual hands on fund raising. The book, *BLACK TIE OPTIONAL: A Complete Special Events Resource for Non-profit Organizations* gives the types of nonprofits that can benefit from one form or another of events.[19] Also these businesses can benefit from just plain old donations from individuals. The monies raised in the

---

[19] Harry A. Freedman, Karen Feldman, *BLACK TIE OPTIONAL: A Complete Special Events Resource for Non-profit Organizations* (Hoboken: John Wiley and Sons Inc., 2007) xvii

previously stated fashion goes to such non-profits as schools, religious institutions, missions, museums, human service agencies, health charities, environmental and animal welfare groups, disaster relief and international aid. Statistically speaking the author of *Black Tie Optional*, Harry Friedman and Karan Feldman reported that in 2007 Americans donated $260.28 billion dollars to some one million charities. Percentage wise it is good to know which grouping of people give the most to charities. The most donors are individuals that give to the tune of 76.5 percent which adds up to 199.07 billion dollars. The balance of the money came from the following donors: corporations 5.3 percent, Foundations 11.5 percent and Bequest 6.7 percent. It is worth the great effort for nonprofits to learn how to get a piece of the pie for their organizations' purposes. Unfortunately statistics show that religious groups used to get 50% of donors' money but since 2004 they only receive 40%. The main reason is because now the other groups are using paid professional fund raisers. Some churches or missions have not caught on to doing that yet. Also, accountability is higher today than it was years before. Many times it takes a professional to demonstrate how the money will be spent as well as, the protocol necessary to continue relationships after monies have been given. In other words what keeps an organization's financial goals flourishing are many repeat donors.

Today the word transparency comes into play especially in instances where there is a financial exchange. In other words transparency in business dealings is the new functioning culture. Non-profits must show concern about ethical standards, have a conflict of interest clause, have audits and make their finances available to the public. Today businesses must also have a whistle blowers protection policy. If errors or any unforeseen misconduct occurs the business will not be destroyed if the appropriate liability clauses in a policy are in effect. The Better Business Bureau has a wise business alliance (www.give.org) that charities should additionally consult. It has guidelines donors expect businesses or churches to follow. Additionally a professional non-profit organization called, "Guide Star," aids in improving the image of charities by requiring their financial statements and practices to be published for public scrutiny. The same businesses should also have their financial dealings and figures on a website of their own. Donors will many times make decisions on who to give to on the basis of what is shown.

Event fundraising for non-profits is another way to raise money. There are many variables. What is appropriate for a particular school, health service, church, disaster relief agency etcetera must be chosen carefully. What can be considered right away is online fund raisings which could use the charities, website in addition to eBay. I am excited about eBay enabling charities to use them because you automatically gain access to 137 million customers! The charity has to sign up with, "Mission Fish" which is a non-profit fundraising partner of eBay. It does accounting for eBay's charity branch. In my estimation it is a wonderful method to raise money so a how to will be given here. An organization must have the following:

a. An email address.
b. An electronic copy of the organization's logo.
c. A forty word mission statement.
d. A voided organization check.
e. Proof of tax exempt status.

Here's the most wonderful part about using them, there is no fee to register and the group gets listed in the eBay, "Giving Works" online directory.

When individual sellers use eBay, specific designated percentage desired to be given to a non-profit charity is given for that sale. Bidders will know that a percentage will be given to a charity because it will be labeled along with the description of the item up for bids.

Groups that qualify can also raise money through having a rummage sale and receive 100 percent of the profit. The items will appear on eBay's, "Giving Works" icon. When the bidding ends the group mails the item directly to the buyers and collects the money. This method is superior to live auctions because the items do not have to be taken anywhere for sale.

Another way to fund an event given by a non-profit business is through the avenue of sponsorship. The book, *Black Tie Optional* spells out the fact that sponsorship is an agreement between local businesses, large corporations or individuals to cover the cost of some aspects of events. Some items covered by sponsors are as follows: invitations to events, food or beverages, entertainment, merchandise, awards and sometimes money. The event promoters feature the sponsor's business in their promotional material and many times also provide specific benefits for the sponsors agreed upon in advance.

In order to get sponsors, you can use business contacts from your own committee to have the event as well as speak to local companies that have full page advertisements in national newspapers and magazines. Much of giving today is due to the desire of companies to market their products and not true philanthropy (Harry A. Freedman and Karen

Feldman). The non-profit has to be more prepared than years ago to give details about how many people will come, and what will be done with their company logo. It is good to have the following information printed for the perspective sponsors to view. The age, income, gender of target markets compared with how this group could possibly match the needs of the desired sponsor. There is something called psychographics which means demonstrating that the products will entice people that have the taste and mannerism to desire the sponsor's products. Additionally, if the non-profit's event is repeated semi-annually or quarterly many sponsors would prefer to give to those events than one that terminates. Businesses like repeated exposure. There is a guide that can aid interested non-profits in obtaining sponsorship called the International Events Group's "Guide to Sponsorship." Additional information about this can be found on www.sponsorship.com.

Thank God, there are those who are mostly philanthropic that agree that there is more to giving than getting back sales for a company. The movie star Paul Newman is spoken of in the book, *Black Tie Optional*, as being an example of a philanthropist that gives one hundred percent of the donor's money to charities. He literally put together a committee of more than one hundred and twenty CEO's and chairpersons to advocate for philanthropy simply because it is good business without getting anything back from the charities. He taught that companies that give with no required amount back are respected by all involved in that company. The included respected persons are shareholders, employees and customers. Paul Newman had a no-strings-attached view of giving to charities which he said, "creates a corporate culture that improves recruiting and retention, extends brand reputation, strengthens inter-employee relationships and reinforces leadership and teamwork." Wow, that was an important point to savor. When I looked at his website called, "Newman's Own," I learned that he has products that he himself sells and gives all of the proceeds to numerous charities. Two of my favorite ones he gives to are Edible School Yard and Clean Water (for countries where people are dying due to drinking polluted water). Newman demonstrated that mass media is more positive when businesses show that they are true philanthropists. When media is positive about a business it increases consumer consumption of their products also. If you remember in an earlier chapter called, *Leadership Traits* I highlighted the author who wrote, *How to Promote Without Being a Jerk's*, theme of persuasion which was to be generous. Here Paul Newman is a prime example of how giving blossoms into great success for businesses that give, expecting nothing directly in return. I call this a positive boomerang effect.

D. Negotiation Used as a Tool to Procure Funding and Outcomes

In Willey Jolley's book, *Turn Setbacks into Greenbacks*, a strategy he presented struck me as a constant aid that will help keep an organization, business or a club funded to a small or large extent. After all, if your resources have plummeted every effort to bring it back up will count. His idea was to use a tool that Americans many times do not use except when buying cars or homes. The apparatus he is speaking of is negotiation.[20] Although, it does not feel directly like it is funding a business, when the chips are down it is definitely a plus. Most business entities see their demise before it hits. The use of negotiation is a proactive way of decreasing negative cash flow in a business. In other words instead of sitting and staring allowing inadequate 'business as usual' practices to continue one must act. Initiating plans of change can make a small or large difference in the sustainability of whatever business venture is involved. Since owners have to buy or sell products anyway if they negotiate, an opportunity door is automatically opened for some positive resource change. Willie Jolley reiterates by giving specific applicable information. "When negotiations take place you can get either a better deal financially or an extra quantity included in the deal." It requires patience and research. It is necessary to study the consumer or loan broker so that you have an understanding about what sensible deal could possibly be made. What comes to my mind is whether the negotiator has something to exchange that could entice a business to reduce their asking price. Jollie puts it this way: See if you can help the manager, or CEO to visualize that looking at the deal through the other's vantage point will positively change their playing field. The manager can visualize that closing a deal with your business can help them grow their own business. Sometimes you can also attempt to get something extra thrown in the deal (An example would be to get an even bigger discount if you consistently use only their store or other type of business). Also it is possible to get an extra

---

[20] Willey Jolley, *Turn Setbacks into Greenbacks* (Hoboken: John Wiley and Sons Inc., 2010) 97, 127, 151

product free for using them. This reminds me of when I was purchasing an expensive bed, the sales man was about to close the deal when I said, 'Aren't you going to give me a free sheet set?' At first he said, "Well the company used to give something but now they do not." He seemed to be crying the recession blues! I was disappointed and my facial expression showed it. "Oh," he suddenly yelled at one of the other employees. "Could you bring her those two pillows, the other customer left?" I received two expensive pillows that I would not have gotten if I were not proactive!

When loans are needed for your business, requests can be made for things like a short delay in having to start repayment. This helped me as a small real estate owner. Imagine what this could do for larger businesses. Businesses can also negotiate for lower installments, interest free or lower interest rates. Instead of accepting a fixed rate mortgage or loan right away a variable rate that has a reasonable maximum cap could be negotiated. The cap prevents the loan interest from ever getting too high. The more proactive a manager or team leader is the greater possibility is for success in landing a deal.

It came to my mind one day that I used to buy insurance from different insurance companies for the few homes that my husband and I owned until I learned a trick of the trade from a contractor friend. He stated that, "If you stick to the same company for all of the homes you will receive a large discount." Bigger businesses should always negotiate for discounts and make a comparison analysis of which company will give them the best deal for the same coverage. At another time a friend recommended an insurance man that turned out to be an insurance wholesaler. His firm did all the calling around on behalf of the consumer and got the best price for the type of required insurance. Think of how much money companies will save for other purposes that will help sustain their businesses year after year if wholesalers are used. Also, when it comes to businesses time economy is synonymous with money. Insurance wholesalers make all the calls, saving businesses hours of research which precludes accomplishing other necessary work.

E. Downsizing as an Alternative to Funding of a Business

Of course a term that is frightening to employees that is helpful for many businesses is downsizing. When businesses prepare their employees by explaining that downsizing is a must for them according to the ups and downs of assets, it will not feel as "cut throat" to the individuals that eventually lose their jobs. No one likes the headache created because of the question, 'How are bills paid without a job?' Since downsizing is a necessity for certain types of businesses, allowing prospective employees to know from the start, that their job will not be completely secure is preventive of very bad outcomes. There will be less anger when managers or team members know the length of their stay in that position will never be written in stone. Having a son who is a systems engineer awakened me to the fact that downsizing is a reality in his trade. He has had various jobs and was usually keeping a job for a period of two to five years and then the company was downsized. The reason why this is being aired is because within three to six months he always got a better job afterwards. One job that downsized had to call him back and give him a raise in order to placate him!

These negative occurrences show that downsizing is a viable method of keeping some companies with positive cash flow.

F. Residual Income Systems; Social Media Advertising; Offering Extra Services; or Contracting Out Jobs, Can All Be Used to Avail Funds

While reviewing my email on my iPad I saw a title utilized by the same women's organization I thought was a waste of my good and limited money. Two marketing experts and authors Wendy Stevens and Nancy Matthews used vocabulary that could and should make marketing products successful. It was called Guerrilla Marketing. I visualized an actual gorilla thrashing his arms and taking control of everything in his immediate environment. This is the aim of a business manager or team leader to take over sales, or projects by being known. As an author I was extremely interested in learning their successful ideals. The word guerrilla takes in all types of entrepreneurial, ventures. So that means it hit your specific area also. These authors gave live training on Guerrilla Marketing. It involves use of YouTube, LinkedIn, and press releases. The information given that can take one to the next level in their project or sales are as follows:

a. Use YouTube to optimize videos.
b. Get leads from LinkedIn by optimizing keywords, video and killer bio.
c. Issue press releases for your business, product or events gaining leads.

The reason these facts are introduced in the funding section of this book is they are low-cost or no cost marketing techniques that greatly stretch exposure of your idea, event or product. These techniques lessen company cost thus heightening financial assets.

Donald Todrin's book *Successfully Navigating the Downturn* revealed a technique that can bring much more income into a small business. His method is called, Service, Service, Service and more Service. His theme of persuasion is service gives you the edge on bigger businesses. It also enhances your ability to compete with other smaller businesses. An addition of various types of services keeps loyal customers even though the business has higher prices than other stores. The reason is people who frequent a store are greater in number than customers who buy everything cheap and are dissatisfied.The services draw a steady customer flow and create an increased cash flow. The type of customers must be known beforehand so that appropriate services will be offered that suit their needs. Now I understand why I used the same store for my Weed Wacker which at times broke. They gave an extended warranty so I could bring it back for repair instead of buying a new one. The business had my name in their computer data base so that it was not necessary to find a many times lost receipt. Here it must be pointed out that convenience keeps customers. It came to mind that, "Full Service," gas stations operate on the same principle. Their gas is priced much higher but when customers that have older cars need help they assist them. They also like full service because of the employee's expertise. Additionally, tools, other equipment and needed products that will keep a car going are sometimes sold in full service garages. The author explained that the cost of these extras that people want is small in comparison to the additional pricing of items that the consumer needs. The following are some of the services that help to fund a business:

1. Free installation.
2. Liberal "no-ask" return policy.
3. Value added design consulting services: the values added extra will encourage buyers to buy more while still in the store.
4. Free assembly: especially, for women who many times are not as handy as men or do not have the strength needed to assemble items purchased, like this feature.
5. Seminars, courses, "how-to" advice on your product or service: this service also will create a desire for purchasing additional items from the store.
6. Telephone support; sometimes consumers buy an appliance such as an adjustable bed and cannot get it to work properly. Technical support diminishes frustration and alleviates anger when the advice gets the item working.
7. Refill reminders.
8. Upgrade services: these latest model services are loved by numerous people who desire every year whatever new innovation is on the market in cell phones, tablets, iPads, laptops as well as DVD players.
9. Free delivery, pick up and removal of the old product: this is definitely desired because your house may be cluttered with an unwanted old appliance because of no help to remove it.

10. Home consultations: home advice is wonderful because the adviser can see just what will fit or look well by actually being in your apartment or home. This advice many times avoid the customer buying an inappropriate item that results in buyer's remorse.
11. Try before you buy service: this is good because some people will keep an item once they tried it even if it is not exactly what they wanted.
12. Information online.
13. Communities and forums through websites, blogs, social networking, Twitter, Facebook, YouTube, etc.: This will keep especially young customers coming back.
14. Foreign language services to bridge barriers: People that cannot speak English well or not at all are happy to pay more in order to get a product that they want as well as understand how it can be used.

The biggest financial blessing I know that can be received by businesses that add various services is word of mouth personal advertising. Excitement and positive exchanges to others about products are accomplished and spread at no cost to the business. The longer these services are in place the more loyal customers can be expected and the more money is made in this manner.

Some may say what does the use of social media or adding services have to do with funding a business. Well, businesses have overhead (rental space, leasing, mortgages, taxes, gas and electricity, water bill, etc.). They also have liabilities (purchasing items to sell, copy machines, printers, computers, paper, phones, intercom systems, furniture, etc.).

Any idea like social media (free or low cost advertisement) that defrays the cost of just running a business in my estimation is funding the business. Entrepreneurs are looking to get the cost of running the business out of the way. After the overhead is taken care of accountants can begin to show them an assets column. Other avenues of borrowing (commercial loans or other types of loans) of course have to be considered. Fund raising or grant writing for a large amount at one time many times has to be approached. Sometimes immediate changes must be implemented right away that may stop foreclosure or bankruptcy proceedings.

As a Speech and Language Pathologist, a lesson learned early on in my career was that therapists can contract themselves out instead of being employed by schools or hospitals directly as staff. When I wanted more money than my salary provided, contracting myself out after school hours became an option. It worked out wonderful at first because I made a full-time salary working two to three evening per week. What happened that took the wind out of my sails was that I did not understand that taxes were not being taken out of my large salary. An accountant spoke to me sharply to my chagrin at the end of the year. He reported that I owed the government sixteen thousand dollars. Indeed that was earth shaking news to me. Of course the next year I saved most of the extra money made from the contract job to pay the previous year's taxes as well as the current year. No employer partial federal or state payroll taxes have to be paid by contractors. Employees are on their honor to pay taxes right away or suffer the consequences.

In the book, *Successfully Navigating The Downturn*, the author had a section dedicated to the benefits and problems with businesses using contractors to work. If it is not a business that contracts out licensed and regulated professionals, the IRS form that has to be submitted leans towards determining all others are employees. The hang-up is as follows. The more control over the proposed independent contractor, the business has the least chance to get the contractor status established. In other words the person will be considered an employee and the application will be denied, if personnel have to be assisted constantly by a supervisor or manager.

The reasons businesses feel the IRS qualifications for contracting out workers should be attempted are more than just the reprieve from paying payroll taxes. Businesses that contract do not have to pay for health insurance, workers' compensation insurance, overtime, holidays, or vacations. It is worth the effort to find out if a business can successfully have contracted out staff due to a giant step into positive cash flow. It is indeed a unique way to get funds into a business by deduction of great cost that most other businesses have to pay for their employees.

It came to my mind that some huge store chains like Lord and Taylor or Macy's buyers sometimes use outsourcing as a cheap method to mass produce suits dresses, coats, lingerie as well as many other commodities that are sold in their stores. How do I know? I read some of the labels in clothing that I purchased from these stores. Even though politicians have used as their platforms many times, "stop outsourcing," in order to encourage consumers to buy products made in the United States there still is not much visible change. The problem is our clothing and many other items are priced an incredible amount higher due to our higher standard of living. Our businesses pay overtime, vacations sick leave, health insurance, partial employee taxes, as well as an extremely higher base salary. I purchased clothing recently and noticed the labels stated that it was made in Malaysia, China or Vietnam. The vast differences in salary for the average worker in these countries create an extremely large demand for American products to be manufactured in these countries. Also they do not have to pay social security or for health insurance for employees. Noticeable at times is some American souvenirs for tourist labels sometimes state ironically that it was made in China or elsewhere. So as far as funding for businesses is concerned, out sourcing makes it possible for many American businesses not only to survive but to become very prosperous.

Reoccurring incomes or what is called residual income funding happens if one involves oneself in certain types of businesses. Movie rentals (Netflix) is one listed on the International Women's Organizations Free Web trainings. Royalties are also given for the sale of published books. Now on College campuses there are *"Express Book Machines."* Students as well as instructors can put money in the machine and a book comes out the same as movie rental machines. I know about these machines because it was included in my publishing package for promotion of my book. It used to be that movies could only be rented in stores but now they can be rented in supermarkets, vacation spots, campuses, and in airports. Whatever vendor rents them gets reoccurring incomes. The movie companies are also recipients of continual royalties. These rentals continue sometimes many decades after the main showing of the movie. The need or desire for cell phone upgrades and accessories also create a reoccurring income. Personally, I have been to Primerica's business presentations and learned that insurance sales brokers survive and some become quite prosperous due to residual income. Every year patrons pay on their insurance policies the sales people receives commissions on their renewal date. So the entrepreneurs business continuously builds through receipt of residual income. The brokers and sales persons also receive bonuses periodically, when they obtain a certain amount of sales. These jobs are actually funded by the business persons own initiatives. In other words the "go getters" make a killing being funded in this manner.

Published books came to my mind to expound upon again because as a new author of my autobiography, I receive royalties from my book quarterly.[21] Even though I must seek new stores, libraries, speaking engagements, book clubs, Facebook, newspapers ads to keep it going. The price of getting the book published does not reoccur. The work is in being proactive and demonstrating excitement in the area of promoting one's own work. The same book will sell without change creating a reoccurring income possibly for many years.

---

21 Velma Osborne, *Autobiography of Velma Osborne Reflects on African-American History* (Bronx, Xulon Press) cover

CHAPTER VII

LEADERSHIP LED PROVIDENTIALLY

A. Positive Effects of Providential Leadership

THE MEANING OF CHRISTIAN leadership differs in that the main thought behind businesses no matter what is the winning of a soul to Christ whenever possible. Additionally, Christian businesses many times have an unusual motive to minister to other's needs according to Roman 15:1. This scripture endorses the attitude of many ministries and some Christian businesses. It states, Pray that I may be kept safe from the unbelievers in Judea and that the contribution I take to Jerusalem may be favorably received by the Lord's people there. In other words building relationships that develop by learning people's needs and showing them love is sometimes more important than accomplishment. What is desired is to be more flexible than secular businesses. Speaking of needs, I remember years ago speaking to a Christian owner of a small pharmacy who was not selling enough medications or receiving reimbursements from Medicaid prescriptions in a timely fashion. Instead of harping on doom or gloom she spoke of getting to talk to her customers about the Lord. Her spirits were high at that time. In other words she was successful according to Matthew 4: 19 at being a fisher of men as well as a mentor as were God's disciples in the Bible. Her agenda was to help people who had various kinds of problems through ministering the word of God as a panacea. In other words she was really functioning as a servant of God showing people that their needs can be met through prayer, serving God and studying his word. Of course this was an example of a Christian business that ended with the owner giving up her franchise. She had to earn her living in a hospital pharmacy and abide by their rules as an employee instead of being a business owner. Even though the secular world looks at an owner like that as a failure she happily gives testimonies about the results of witnessing to people when she owned a pharmacy.

When a reflection is given from a faithful Christian it is void of their personal passions, whims and manias. Consideration of the other person has become paramount. Today is a time that from childhood Americans in general are taught to be individuals to the extent that some of them use cut throat techniques in business. Staff seminars or workshops may call it hard sell or some other term. This devious practice tricked an incredible amount of people. An example of what happens when some people in the higher echelon of business are free to follow their greedy passions, took place when the Federal Reserve took away their strict restraints on procuring mortgages.[22] CEO's of banks and investment houses charged variable rate interest loans, that had extremely high caps (means interest rates went higher and higher every year). So after the three year low rate ended, the new rates kept on rising and became unattainable for the home owners. Others in the general population were manipulated into buying homes they could not afford because of no-money down contracts (subprime mortgages). Individuals were literally yanked into deals that were not affordable in the long run. Others were swindled into getting interest only loans for three years but at the end of that time they had to pay both interest and the principle to the mortgager (balloon mortgages). Since millions of individuals were lured into these predatory, hook types of loans a boomerang affect challenged our entire nation's economy. Real-estate sales representatives received large bonuses for procuring unaffordable mortgages from the general population, (which was an enticement). The brokerage houses employing theses sales persons became very wealthy on the backs of others. Most people did not have the understanding of the repercussions of entering into what really were contracts that only the wealthy could fulfill. Leading bankers became extremely wealthy as millions began to lose their homes, pensions, savings and credit ratings. It was the main cause of the 2007 stock market crash. The resulting recession was mostly due to the creation of an artificial buyers' market! What I call deals that

---

22 Gretchen Morgenson, *How the Thundering Herd Faltered and Fell* (The New York Times 9 Nov. 2008: BU) 1, 9

"backfired" were so severe that many independent adults lost their homes and had to move in with their children. Retired people had to go back to work. Some others had to go to food pantries in order to eat. These horrific results of these immoral transactions were dealt with in this book to exemplify the Christian belief that the love of money is sinful and not an option. First Timothy chapter six verses ten confirms the results. It reads, "For the love of money is a root of all kinds of evil. Some people, eager for money, have wandered from the faith and pierced themselves with many grieves."

What happened after the results of predatory loans that was apparent was mass media made a circus out of those that perpetrated the business of manipulating others for their own gain. Many were put under public scrutiny that was mortifying to those who enacted the crimes. Next the Occupy Wall Street demonstrators came on the scene and created a seven day of the week four to five weeks per month reminder. What was desired were jobs, return of properties, and stoppage of huge bonuses bank officials awarded each other by approving unworkable loans and other unscrupulous dealings. A reappearance of the disappearing middle class was preferred. Much negative attention was given to the greedy leaders of these monetary establishments. Practicing Christians that hold offices believe it is a "must" to guard against becoming spiritually or mentally hardened. Saints must not be so bureaucratic that feeling for others dissipate. This means that the saints in leadership should have empathy for others and not take advantage of them for filthy lucre or any other reason.

What should be considered a standard in providential leadership is what could be called development of leaders under a chief leader. These carefully chosen persons should be first loyal to God. Next they should be able to handle every aspect of the church, mission, youth or senior center. The importance of having a continuum of service in Christian spheres of influence is imperative. In other words if someone has family problems is sick or dies the services, recreational activities or missions should not stop. Delegation of authority should be carried through consistently. The spreading of responsibilities takes work overload off the heads of departments, Bishops, Pastors, or Ministers that lead auxiliaries. This belief should be taken into privately owned businesses led by believers in the Lord Jesus Christ. Delegating authority is really a Biblically sound doctrine. Moses in the book of Exodus passed his knowledge unto Joshua. David passed his charge onto Solomon. Consulting with Dr. Sotilleo in "New Greater Bethel Bible Institute," I received the following information, "Succession in the apostolic faith carries this concept. The apostolic fathers passed the baton to the church fathers and the church fathers preserved the teaching of Jesus Christ for us." The bottom line to remember is to prayerfully put potential leaders with experienced leaders for apprenticeship training. The morale on the job will be higher because of their new responsibilities. Their newly developed abilities may have to be fully used when emergencies or added duties are required. Also these new leaders provide insurance against churches, church programs or missions shutting down when auxiliary heads, pastors or managers cannot perform any longer. Church doors will not be permanently closed due to a Pastor's death or incompetence.

Getting into the main thrust of Christian leadership that is also financially viable, the structure is as follows according to Dr. Sotilleo's list paraphrased and explained here.

1. A leader is a guide who helps his staff, team, and committee, or auxiliary, to reach desired objectives, and get a worthwhile job done well. This requires persistence, and determination, and initiative of the leader to sometimes go beyond the duties that are required. The follower is loyal to the leader because the follower has noticed his own growth personally because of a caring leader.
2. The Christian leader's commitment must be inclusive of integrity. In other words they must be able to keep a secret. They must not give false excuses instead of completing work. He or she must also surmount the most challenging problem that a Christian leader encounters which is sharing the same vision as the Pastor of the church. Sharing the same vision means you cannot switch to an idea that you like better or that would work better for you. For example funds cannot be placed in foreign missions because there is a greater need there than to renovate the church! You must work with the leader's vision because he sees the gestalt of the picture. You only see a fraction of it. The church may own other properties or investments that will eventually produce funds for foreign missions at a later date or never. Or he may have a plan to build a school or other community development that you do not know will be implemented later. The Pastor's vision must be kept until you are given your own vision and separate from that church. The reason can be remembered in mathematical terms. A part can never be larger than a whole!

3. A leader has to have the ability to make policies, administrate, develop programs, as well as discharge sometimes difficult responsibilities to the followers.
4. Church leadership programs should not be primarily social and should not be political or worldly. The leader should be leading according to Deuteronomy 8:18.

   "[18] But thou shalt remember the Lord thy God; for it is He that giveth thee power to get wealth." It should be added that moral restrictions keep away contentions that other businesses struggle with or are destroyed by successful whistle blowers.
5. Church leaders are concerned about having:
   a. Fellowship committee leaders.
   b. Recreation Leaders.
   c. Welcoming /Hospitality Committees.
   d. Leaders that are property owners that can serve as trustees.
   e. Care and Maintenance Committees.
   f. Finance Department Leaders that function in the following areas:
      i. Chairman of Current Expenses.
      ii. Chairman of Benevolence.
      iii. Treasurer for each fund.
      iv. Auditing Committee.
      v. Wills and Bequests Committee.
      vi. Building Fund Committee.

g. Minister in Membership-training class.
h. Qualified Christian Counselor or Pastoral Counselor.
i. Community Outreach leader for Social Welfare and Action.
j. Leader of Midweek Prayer Service.
k. Chairman of Publicity.
l. Chief Usher and Assistants.

All of these divisions are not usually in one church. Also denominations differ as to what positions should be emphasized or exist in their church.

In the book entitled, *Turn Setbacks into Greenbacks*, there are three F's for success. Since Jolley has the *Willie-Jolley Motivational Minute* heard in fifty markets, and has a *National News Press Association* column with a six figure readership on the internet, I know his opinion is valuable. The 3 F's that he emphasizes are Faith, Focus, and Follow through! His theme of persuasion is, "You must pray first, believe and apply your faith with actual action." In other words you have to keep the momentum going in order to turn your setbacks into greenbacks. Don't drop the ball and regret it later. Dropping the ball is due to being consumed with fear in my estimation. Jolley mentioned that fear is false evidence appearing to an individual as being real. II Timothy 1:7 confirms, "…for God hath not given us the spirit of fear; but of power, and of love, and of a sound mind." Rejection of an idea or product you have by even one person can frighten you out of speaking to anyone else about it. Sometimes finding out why someone turned you down will demonstrate a reason for you to go forward full blast. It could be because they are too busy. It could be there is no way they can use your idea or product but a few thousand others can. It could be plain old jealousy. For this reason prayer has to be increased to surmount fear, so you can present what you have to numerous people and stop taking no for a final answer.

Another scenario that can be compared to the grim reaper is depression regardless of the cause. Managing the church business or outreach ministry was going well but a private problem created personality discord. Complaining about the various boards and auxiliaries and team leaders in the church begins to take center stage. Procrastination sets in and instead of quickly getting business accomplished time is being wasted. Excuses begin to replace exuberance.

What can be done about the depressive feelings that are now like the weight of a saddle upon a human? Repetitive complaining has been unproductive. Negativity is being seen in many areas of the job as an overseer of various departments in the church. Corrupting thoughts are beginning to take over where a balanced analysis of situations used to be. Complaining is driving people away. What can be done to eradicate a defeatist attitude? Sometimes getting away from people who do not have positive attitudes is necessary. For yourself take time out for relaxation. Exercise or get your hair done if you are a woman. Listen to worship music. Read scriptures that are relevant or a panacea for your particular emotional dilemmas. Thinking of the last part of the Lord's Prayer can be helpful. A request is made to God, "Deliver us from evil for thine is the kingdom and the power and the Glory! (KJV)". Also this song comes to my mind that also has a scripture bases.

I will do a new thing in you
I will do a new thing in you
Whatever you ask for
Whatever you need
That I will not deny
Saith the Lord
Saith the Lord

The scriptural base for this song is found in Isaiah 43:19. It exalts, "Behold, I will do a new thing; now it shall spring forth; shall ye not know it? I will even make a way in the wilderness, *and* rivers in the desert." I tell you just writing this anointed Rhema word delights me. When you are involved in church business transmission of joy as well as a serious countenance at times is a mandate for positive transference to staff.

When I joined a woman's organization as a new author of my autobiography book, I thought I made a mistake. Why did I do this I inquired of myself? It's another mistake. It's not for someone like me. Perhaps I thought this is for female politicians, women libbers, boutique owners, Directors of schools, salon or spa owners. It turned out that a very interesting lesson was to be learnt by me and for a certainty numerous others. Here is a paraphrase from a lesson I learned from the Woman's Prosperity Network with my own fruitful twist. People who consistently complain many times have to be compliant to the very conditions in which they are in opposition. The reason is there is very often no solution contained in their complaints. The Bible decrees in John 15:7-8 "If ye abide in me, and my words abide in you, ye shall ask what ye will, and it shall be done unto you.[8] Herein is my Father glorified, that ye bear much fruit; so shall ye be my disciples."The above is what Cindy

Trimm who is listed among Ebony's Magazines power one hundred doers and influencers, considers spoken declarations that activate God's power.[23] After declaring your desire or need you should ask the Father to give you new ideas from the auxiliaries, committees, team leaders or finance board through feedback or reflections at the end of meetings, written instructions or job executions. What I have to do to advance in my personal business that will help others is call one of the liaisons at the Women's organization I joined. An inquiry can be made by me as to how I could promote my motivational book. It is inclusive of my progression and success in life through Biblical teachings in the church and seminary. Perhaps I can network through them and have my book added to some of their member's book clubs. Possibly I could receive a speaking engagement or a book signing through some of their connections. All of these ideas came to me after months of no personal contact with anyone in the organization. I now am cognizant of the fact that I should not get depressed or down-casted. All believers must pray that your personal ventures, succeed by God giving you favor with people that can propel you forward. You are not a lone ranger when you have God on your side. Those Pastors, Bishops or their designees that lead or manage church functions or outreaches (including church bookstores) will advance also by asking for the favor of God to intercede on their behalf. Reading an appropriate scripture on a daily basis will arrest errors on your part.

Two of the scriptures of positive disposition are as follows: Matthew 6:10a, "Thy will be done on earth as it

---

23 Cindy Trimm, *Commanding Your Morning!* (USA: Charisma House, 2007) ii

is in heaven." Next you say to yourself, what is his will for me? God's grace abounds toward you in III John 1:2. It exalts, "Beloved, I wish above all things that thou mayest prosper and be in health, even as thy soul prospereth (KJV)." In others words you must come out of self because of your imperfections and depend on God and prosper. The other advancement scripture is taken from Joel 2:24, "The threshing floors shall be full of wheat, and the vats shall overflow with new wine and oil." Resist temptation to voice negative thoughts or ideas, after you pray. Thank God for the positive changes in your personal endeavors, the church, its programs or outreaches, and give God praise!

Pressure, it affects all businesses including church businesses which are at times incorporated [501(c)(3)]. Since our country (USA) went into a recession in 2009 churches as well as most other businesses had to function on a much smaller budget. Many churches that have mortgages or high rents that were paid by tithes and offerings given to the church received much less due to members losing jobs; some only working part-time and some accepting job concessions including big cuts in their salaries. Others lost their pensions and nest egg that they were building for their future. This is a good place to mention Willie Jolley's word focus as one of the necessities for an organization or individual to be successful. I read an article written by Robert Kennedy which stated that, "An organization is a group of people that are tasked to move towards a common goal. It is only the problem of how to get everyone unified that has to be conquered."

The limitations imposed by dealing with smaller budgets can be conquered in some of these ways given below. A way to get information to the young people in the church free or for very little money is the use of automatic posting of various fund raisers, outreach events, gospel concerts or revivals through the use of Facebook. Leaders can get youth together for seminars or brief instructions on Skype. Of course e-mail can be used to advise members of all ages that are computer literate via email. Colorful flyers, for all events can be attached to emails and printed out at no cost to the church. The general congregation members can receive e-mails also for revivals, health clinics, fund raisers, fellowship luncheons, dinners or prayer breakfasts. Of course reminders of important events or services are also announced at services, choir rehearsals, Bible studies as well as posted on bulletin boards for all to peruse. It is also necessary to teach the older members that have not grown up with computers the importance of learning how to e-mail and use a least one or two social connectors. It is wise to have dates of trainings and advise middle aged and senior people what to buy if they do not have a laptop or tablet or a cell that can receive text and e-mail.

Leaders of youth groups can keep fellowship going for young people by use of Skype, FaceTime, Instagram, Facebook, Twitter, blogs and other social media connectors. Leaders of the groups need to advise the young people what not to put on social media due to identity theft, bullying or the possibility of other types of misdemeanors, or felony crimes. Young people should also be advised to delete any inappropriate sharing or postings by others that were sent to them. The public that visits the site may believe this is the warped way that the owner of the site thinks! It is necessary with youth to make a date for feedback to review which social media sites are the most beneficial as far as the purposes that were outlined. This will give the leaders the ability later to spread the word about what the best social media sites are and for what specific purposes!

Epilogue

Seven chapters have been presented in order that teams, managers, project heads, family and faith-based organizations, stores, other businesses, health facilities, and school administrators will make beneficial changes. Students will get an understanding about leadership and how to start up a business in the future if they desire. It has been shown that due to today's high accountability, it is mandatory for businesses to hire a consultant. Transparency is the call of today. Consultants eliminate costly errors as well as legal problems. Consultants also help businesses to compete with other similar firms. Baby boomers used to go to a general practitioner for everything years ago, but today is the era of the specialist. You receive referrals from your primary care provider and have to many times go to several different specialist. Drawing a parallel to businesses, 'no matter how successful they are there is always an area that could use tweaking.' Ideas from consultants aid in the formation of a continuum of success. Changes in quality of life as well as increased income have been projected for all that read this book. Improvements are not to be limited only to their personal endeavors, but additionally to society.

Bibliography

Barsh, Joanna and Johanne Lavoie, *Centered Leadership: Leading with Purpose* (New York: Crown Publishing 2014) 156-167

Bradberry, Travis and Jean Greaves, *Learn the Secret of Adaptive Leadership* (San Diego: Talent Smart 2012) 190

Erickson, Millard J., *Christian Theology* (Grand Rapids: Bakers Academic a Division of Baker Publishing Group, 1998) 1079-1084

Freedman, Harry A., and Karen Feldman, *BLACKTIE OPTIONAL: A Complete Special Events Resource for Non-profit Organizations* (Hoboken: John Wiley and Sons Inc., 2007) xvii

Freud Ann, *The Ego and the Mechanism of Defense* (London, Kornac Books 1966) 59

Geiser Jill, *Work Happy: What Great Bosses Know* (NYC: Center Street: Hachette Book Group, 2012) 29

Hewlett Sylvia Ann, *Top Talent: Keeping Performance up When Business is Down* (Boston: Harvard Business Press, 2009) 78-81

Hilbert-Davis, Jane and W. Gibb Dyer, Jr. *Consulting to Family Businesses: A Practical Guide to Contracting, Assessment, and Implementation* (San Francisco, Pfeiffer a Wiley Imprint) 24, 100

Holy Bible: KJV (USA Thomas Nelson Bibles /a Division of Thomas Nelson Inc.) 358, 467, 596

Hyun Jane, and Audrey S. Lee, *Flex the New Playbook for Managing Across Differences* (New York: Harper Collins 2014) xxvi

Jamail Nathan, *The Leadership Playbook to Build Winning Teams: Creating a Culture of Winning Business Teams* (New York: Build Penguin Group 2014) 80

Jolly Wiley, *Turn Setbacks into Greenbacks* (Hoboken: John Wiley and Sons Inc. 2010) 97, 127, 151

Jordan Bernard, *Spiritual Protocol* (NY Zoey Publishing 1994) 20

Kasanoff Bruce, *How to Self-Promote Without Being a Jerk* (WestPoint: Now Possible, 2014) i-iv

Mandela Nelson, *Long Walk to Freedom: The Autobiography of Nelson Mandela* (New York: Little Brown and Co., 1995) 379

Maxwell John, *Developing the Leader within You* (Nashville: Thomas Nelson, 2005) 1

Merriam Webster Dictionary (Philippines: Webster Inc., 1995)

Morgenson Gretchen, *How the Thundering Herd Faltered and Fell* (The New York Times 9 Nov. 2008: BU) 1, 9

Osborne Velma, *Autobiography of Velma Osborne Reflects on African-American History* (Bronx, Xulon Press) cover

Papadakis Maxine A, *Current Medical Diagnoses and Treatment* (USA: McGraw Hill-Education, 2012) 174

Poza Ernesto J., *Family Business* (Mason: South Western Cengage Learning, 2010) 244

Shambaugh Rebecca, *Make Room for Her* (USA: Mcgraw Hill, 2013) 20, 24

Silverman Debbie and Trish Carr, *It's Just a Conversation: What to Say and How to Say It in Business* (Chicago: Parker House Books 2014)

Todrin Donald, *Successfully Navigating the Downturn: Economic and Competitive Survival Strategies* (Madison: Jere Calmes 2011) 54, 138, 139

Trimm Cindy, *Commanding Your Morning!* (USA: Charisma House, 2007) 4

Widener Chris, *Leadership Rules: How to Become a Leader You Want to Be* (CA: A Wiley Imprint, 2011), 45

www.ingramcontent.com/pod-product-compliance
Lightning Source LLC
Chambersburg PA
CBHW031901200326
41597CB00012B/510

* 9 7 8 1 9 4 9 3 6 2 9 3 0 *